ANTHROPOLOGY AND CONSULTANCY

STUDIES IN APPLIED ANTHROPOLOGY
General Editor: Sarah Pink, University of Loughborough

Anthropology and Consultancy: Issues and Debates
Edited by Pamela J. Stewart and Andrew Strathern

In preparation
Applications of Anthropology: Professional Anthropology in the
Twenty-first Century
Edited by Sarah Pink

ANTHROPOLOGY AND CONSULTANCY

Issues and Debates

Edited by

Pamela J. Stewart

and

Andrew Strathern

Berghahn Books
NEW YORK • OXFORD

Published in 2005 by
Berghahn Books

www.berghahnbooks.com

Library of Congress Cataloging-in-Publication Data

Anthropology and consultancy : issues and debates / edited by Pamela J.
Stewart and Andrew Strathern.
     p. cm. — (Studies in applied anthropology)
The papers collected for this book are a special issue of "Social Analysis".
Includes bibliographical references.
ISBN 1-57181-552-X (alk. paper)
     1. Applied anthropology. 2. Anthropologists. 3. Consultants.
I. Stewart, Pamela J. II. Strathern, Andrew. III. Social analysis
(Adelaide, S. Aust.). Special number. IV. Series.

GN397.5.A567 2004
301—dc22

2004056001

British Library Cataloguing in Publication Data

A catalogue record for this book is available from
the British Library.

Printed in Canada on acid-free paper

CONTENTS

PREFACE

Anthropologists, and presumably other investigators of social processes, are often faced with a tension between understanding problems and suggesting ways of dealing with those problems. The problems in question may be theoretical or practical, and ways of dealing with them may vary from simply writing about them to being employed directly as an agent to bring putative or actual "solutions" to a local population. The issues of "whose problems" and "whose solutions" are bound to arise in such contexts. The category "applied anthropology" has been used to demarcate the work of anthropologists when they specifically attempt to apply their knowledge in order to bring about changes in people's perceived situations. Most notably, these changes have occurred first under the conditions of colonialism and subsequently in post-colonial situations where various kinds of development are being introduced, are planned, or have already come into being. A considerable literature has developed around this enterprise.

Writings on applied anthropology tend to fall into one or other of two groupings: one is the "how to do it" genre of manuals and textbooks for practitioners who will be trained to make applied work their career. The other belongs to critical anthropology, with its focus on critiques of colonialism, imperialism, capitalism, and exploitative aspects of development generally. One genre tells readers how best to carry it out, the other marshals arguments essentially against doing it at all, perhaps without offering any concrete alternatives. There is, however, a more nuanced stream of work that tries to be critically aware of wider contexts while at the same time seriously discussing engagement with specific pieces of work and what can be learned from them. Such pieces of work may involve short-term consultancies or longer-term studies. The ethnographic method has itself been invoked in order to gain a reasonable overview, for example, of how aid agencies around the world actually operate (Crewe and Harrison 1998; see also Stirrat 2000 on "Cultures of Consultancy"). Anthropologists

References for this section begin on page xii.

who have a long-term knowledge of a particular region have sometimes turned to an assessment of the problems surrounding development in that region, using their experience to do so, as Victor King has done for South-East Asia, particularly Malaysia and Indonesia (King 1999). Especially in fields such as medical anthropology that intersect with the work of health care personnel, the value of the anthropologist's perspective is well recognized (Frankel and Lewis 1989; King 1999:214–238). In some instances the anthropologist's involvement may arise out of long-term biographical experience. Gideon Kressel, writing on his long-term work with Bedouin pastoralists in the Negev region of Israel, begins his account with his childhood memories of seeing Bedouin "herds, campsites, and tents" and his later time as "a young shepherd" at a kibbutz in 1951–1952. His interest in the adaptive preservation of Bedouin pastoralist ways and the role of applied anthropology in interfacing between these pastoralists and the state is underpinned by his concern for the shepherds. He notes, for instance, that the shepherds are not equipped to pursue complaints against government officials, who use the power of the state to override them (Kressel 2003:xiii, 77). (See also Raz 2004 for an applied medical anthropology study of this same Bedouin population.)

Debates about applied anthropology are closely interwoven in general with debates about development anthropology and the anthropology of development (Willigen 2002), and about modernization theory and the whole concept of "modernity". Katy Gardner and David Lewis have reviewed the demise of general modernization theory and the monolithic assumptions regarding inevitable trends toward modernity that it entailed, proposing that we reconsider applied anthropology in the light of "the post-modern challenge" (Gardner and Lewis 1996; see also Grillo and Rew 1985 for an earlier study of comparable issues and Mars 2004 for a contemporary overview). Essentially, this involves responding to the heterogeneity and specificity of situations where applied anthropologists work, giving full recognition to the conjunctural forces involved but also to the agencies of the people who are intimately involved in the development policies, sometimes as the targets but sometimes as consultants. Recognition of agency may also merge into advocacy (and Kressel's work, cited above, has a clear element of advocacy in it, backed up by intensive long-term research). Gardner and Lewis note the pitfalls that may be involved in advocacy; but they also note that this role has nowadays often been appropriated by non-governmental organizations (NGOs), and by community groups themselves. "Sustainable development" is often a focus of such groups, in opposition to outside developers. The Earthwatch Institute is an example of a foundation that is a non-profit international organization devoted to promoting policies and actions that they define as being conducive to a sustainable environment generally. A classic example of how mainstream anthropological work can imply a need to alter policy without having to advocate this directly comes from work by John Grayzel, who worked with FulBe pastoralists in rural Mali in Africa. Grayzel showed that while FulBe herd management generally followed so-called rational principles of maximizing livestock production, there were individual variations in behavior, which he was able convincingly to relate to the FulBe value of *pulaade*, centered on ideas of "intelligence, beauty, wealth, and independence". These cultural values meant that policies of development planners that did not take them into account were likely to produce false predictions and to fail (cited in Nolan 2002:12–13).

The lessons implied in the instances given above reinforce the point that applied anthropology is an extension of anthropological work in general. It is not a marked sub-field, although it may represent a specific professional vocation. (Mars 2004 argues that applied anthropology should be integrated more into the work of departments in the U.K. Interestingly, he cites the theoretical work of Mary Douglas on perceptions of risk as having stimulated the work of professionals in the applied sphere.) In certain contexts anthropologists have been drawn increasingly into applied work. This is notably the case in Australasia, and perhaps most markedly in the case of Aboriginal studies in Australia, where the legal decisions granting land rights to Aboriginal populations unleashed a flood of problems relating to the determination of who had authentic claims to particular stretches of land. All the theoretical and ethnographic debates that anthropologists had engaged in for half a century or more among themselves found their way into this new context, and applied pieces of work have become a stock-in-trade of many specialists on Aboriginal studies in Australia since then (see, for example, the studies in Rumsey and Weiner 2001 and in Toussaint and Taylor 1999). The sources of funding for such studies clearly impact their terms of reference and outcomes. Strenuous arguments occur about the validity or otherwise of testimonies regarding "ownership" of resources (e.g. Peace 2003; Povinelli 1993; Weiner 1999, 2001). These arguments in turn tend to reflect political and ideological positions as well as questions of objectivity in anthropology as a "science" (Keen 1999, in the volume edited by Sandy Toussaint and Jim Taylor, reviews this question in the context of applied anthropology).

Anthropologists working in Papua New Guinea have been confronted by applied issues with particular sharpness in relation to mining projects which can bring large influxes of cash to populations but also precipitate severe social problems and entail considerable displacements of people. As with the Australianists, anthropologists, specializing in Papua New Guinea have often been brought in to determine who has rights in relation to land and who therefore should receive compensation or royalties from mining operations. Since mines may cause environmental pollution and are certainly suspected of doing so, ethical and ecological issues are intertwined here. The volume of studies edited by Alan Rumsey and James Weiner (2001) explores this terrain of work in depth. The anthropologists who contributed to this volume tended to be long-term professionals whose ethnographic knowledge pre-dated the mining projects at stake or was independent of their work on these projects. They were not "applied anthropologists" but undertook pieces of applied work, or were commenting on such pieces of work, from their own knowledge-bases and their own intellectual positions. The question of whose knowledge is involved comes strongly to the fore in two chapters on competing versions of "land ownership" in the region of the Nena mining project. Dan Jorgensen pertinently asks, "Who and what is a landowner?" (Jorgensen 2001; on similar issues among the Duna people, see Stewart and Strathern 2002). Don Gardner, dealing with the same case, looks into the deeper philosophical background in the people's own ideas about "truth", including the idea reported by Jorgensen that "the indeterminacy of the world transcends human knowledge" (Gardner 2001:117)—which would make debates about who really holds claims to land ultimately moot and also makes of the Telefolmin people something resembling post-modernists. More generally, the bureaucratic and political concept of exclusive land ownership impinges awkwardly on the fluid complexities of New Guinea ideas, adapted to a world of local movements and overlapping claims to resources. The problem arises from the conjuncture of sharply different regimes of political economy and mythology. The mythological contexts are delineated further by Wardlow and Ernst in the same volume (Ernst 2001; Wardlow 2001); Bill Sagir examines emergent local politics in the context of petroleum extractions at Lake Kutubu (Sagir 2001); and Stuart Kirsch explores the experiential dimensions of the impact of pollution from the Ok Tedi mine on the Yonggom people (Kirsch 2001). "The land" in these contexts has to be understood in its full experiential and mythologically established senses in which land and human bodies are linked together in cyclical fashion (Stewart and Strathern 2001a, 2002). Applied anthropology comes full circle with interpretive anthropology here.

Closing circles in this way provides options for anthropological workers, who may be hired for short-term applied projects or engaged in longer-term ethnographic work. Our collection of essays in this volume is designed specifically to demonstrate the practical efforts of ethnographers who are faced with a variety of concerns in their field areas that raise issues that are debated within the field of research itself. This collection is also particularly intended to show the links and similarities, as well as the disjunctures and dissimilarities, between different contexts of ethnographic work, and therefore to break down artificial dichotomies such as "pure" versus "applied" work. Our aim has been to create a level playing field for the debates surrounding consultancy, not to arbitrate between players in terms of "high" or "low" ground (*pace* Bastin and Morris 2003:78). We stress the point that, in practical terms, ethnographic work is inevitably involved with the world at large and with the forces that work in it (see, for example, Harper 2002); while we also point to some particular conditions that constrain the special world of consultancy work (see again Janes 2003 and Stirrat 2000). Equally, the studies that we present in this collection recognize the contingency and the variety of issues a consultancy project may entail, while pointing to numbers of generalities that are involved.

Our primary aim in this collection was to provide a forum where anthropologists engaged in the practice of their work, using this term in a broad sense, could reflect on the implications of their position either as consultants in the immediate context, or as ethnographers working in an environment occupied by collective consultancy organizations such as NGOs. Interestingly, one of the essays published here, by Paige West, which discusses her experience of working in the same area of the Papua New Guinea Highlands where an environmental NGO had a project for wildlife management, won the American Anthropological Association's Anthropology and Environment Junior Scholar Award. West's discussion is substantive, critical, and reflexive, as are the other fine essays presented here which bring an insightful range of perspectives to bear on the topic.

Essays that have been published after our collection first appeared as a special issue of *Social Analysis* in 2001 (Stewart and Strathern 2001b) have in many ways followed our lead by presenting reflective practical experiences. For example, Craig Janes, a well-known epidemiologist who has done much to broaden the scope of epidemiology in the direction of ethnography, discusses attempts made between himself and an Asian Development Bank (ADB) professional officer to resolve his criticisms regarding the impact of ADB-sponsored reforms on the health care system in Mongolia (Janes 2003). George Henrikson outlines the work of the International Work Group for Indigenous Affairs, noting difficulties with the term "indigenous" here (Henrikson 2003:117), and he goes on to reflect upon his own work with the Innu nation on documenting their land use patterns in order to secure their rights to the land, and his later involvement in claims relating to a mining project in their area. He stresses the difficult situations of both the Innu and himself as their consultant in between various state and commercial organizations (pp. 119–121). And he recognizes, finally, the dangers that may be involved in advocacy: "the consultant, perhaps building on the vision that the indigenous people have for their future, may come to create aspirations that are wholly unrealistic, and therefore in the end both dangerous and destructive" (p. 122).

Steven Robins also takes up the question of working with "indigenous peoples", in his case study of resettled San communities in South Africa (2003). He was commissioned by the Africa-Pacific-Caribbean/European Union to write a report that would give credit to the South African government and would also advance the claims of these San people to international donor funding. He asked himself if a report which "detailed San involvement in modern warfare and strategies of state terror that tainted romantic images of 'the harmless people' living close to nature" would be congenial to potential donors and indigenous peoples NGOs (Robins 2003:131). He goes on to discuss the roles of NGOs in general "in local political processes, in mediating representations of the San, and in brokering global discourses on 'civil society'" (p. 132). Rival NGOs engaged in turf wars, and San communities were split between those advocating "traditional culture" versus those arguing for the adoption of "Western ideas and practices" (ibid.). Robins aptly calls these contexts and processes "NGO culture wars".

The arguments about culture in general that have preoccupied anthropologists in their theoretical debates thus find their replicas and simulacra in a transmogrified domain, that of the aid agencies and NGOs themselves. The studies in our collection here discuss these dilemmas in nuanced and reflective ways. While fieldwork cannot by itself solve the problems that occur in contemporary contexts, it is an essential precondition for reflecting on and understanding them, and hence of providing more thoughtful ways of approaching them in future. (This includes research done by those from outside of the group[s] under study and those from inside the group[s] being studied.) *Experientia docet.*

One relatively new strand of work on the problems of development reinforces the point that detailed fieldwork, while not necessarily presenting clear solutions to these problems, is essential to making an approach to such solutions. This is the strand known as indigenous knowledge (IK) studies. Here indigenous knowledge stands in much the same semantic space as terms like "culture" or "value orientations" have done in previous times. The basic proposition is that better understanding of the practical workings and scope of the indigenous knowledge of topics such as forest growth, soils, plant types, livestock patterns, cultivation processes, and the like, must surely help to create an interface between local people and introduced forms of technological development based on forms of knowledge from outside sources. In a broader sense, all kinds of culturally established "knowledge" may be relevant to the development process, and this is why local people need to be an integral part of programs and projects in their areas. In one of the recent volumes devoted to an exposition of the IK approach (Bicker, Sillitoe, and Pottier 2004; see also Ellen, Parkes, and Bicker 2000; Sillitoe 2000; and Sillitoe, Bicker, and Pottier 2002), we have also pointed to the significance of mythological knowledge (*malu*) among the Duna people of Papua New Guinea, giving them a way of negotiating for compensation and royalties from the Porgera Joint Venture gold-mining operation (Stewart and Strathern 2004). What is at stake here is not whether such knowledge is in all respects "ancient" or "authentic", but how it is developed and presented as a performance in contemporary interactions. Whether knowledge is "hybrid", "pure", "ancient", or "invented", what matters is the efficacy of such knowledge in processes of negotiation about development and conservation issues, as Colin Filer argues (Filer 2004). The IK approach is not a means to obviate or nullify the many difficulties that applied anthropology encounters in the field of development, many of which difficulties result from power differentials beyond the control of the anthropologists and the people with whom they work. Its value, however—and this is a very considerable value—lies in its insistence that significant knowledge, whether technical or symbolic, does not belong only to the developers, but rather is found importantly, and often crucially, among those who are locally most impacted by development projects. Here again the general orientations of the ethnographer and the requirements of the applied anthropologist come full circle with each other. If a problem has a solution, it is in the details of the case studied, and in the imaginative insights that are brought to bear on these details.

Acknowledgments

We would like to express our appreciation to Berghahn Books for working with us on this publication. We are very pleased that this book is part of Berghahn's new Studies in Applied Anthropology series.

— *Andrew Strathern and Pamela J. Stewart*

References

Bastin, Rohan and Barry Morris 2003 "Introduction to Forum". *Social Analysis* 47(1):77–83.

Bicker, Alan, Paul Sillitoe, and Johan Pottier (eds) 2004 *Development and Local Knowledge: New Approaches to Issues in Natural Resource Management, Conservation, and Agriculture*. London and New York: Routledge.

Crewe, Emma and Elizabeth Harrison 1998 *Whose Development? An Ethnography of Aid*. London and New York: Zed Books.

Ellen, Roy, Peter Parkes, and Alan Bicker (eds) 2000 *Indigenous Environmental Knowledge and Its Transformations*. Amsterdam: Harwood.

Ernst, T.M. 2001 "Land, Stories and Resources: Some Impacts of Large-Scale Resource Exploitation on Onabasulu Lifeworlds". In Alan Rumsey and James Weiner (eds) *Mining and Indigenous Lifeworlds in Australia and Papua New Guinea*, pp. 125–144. Adelaide: Crawford House Publishing

Filer, Colin 2004 "The Knowledge of Indigenous Desire: Disintegrating Conservation and Development in Papua New Guinea". In Alan Bicker, Paul Sillitoe, and Johan Pottier (eds) *Development and Local Knowledge: New Approaches to Issues in Natural Resource Management, Conservation, and Agriculture*, pp. 64–92. London and New York: Routledge.

Frankel, Stephen and Gilbert Lewis (eds) 1989 *A Continuing Trial of Treatment: Medical Pluralism in Papua New Guinea*. Boston: Kluwer Academic Publishers.

Gardner, Katy and David Lewis 1996 *Anthropology, Development and the Post-Modern Challenge*. London: Pluto Press.

Grillo, Ralph and Alan Rew (eds) 1985 *Social Anthropology and Development Policy*. ASA Monograph no. 23. London and New York: Tavistock.

Harper, Janice 2002 *Endangered Species: Health, Illness and Death among Madagascar's People of the Forest*. Durham, N.C.: Carolina Academic Press.

Henrikson, Georg 2003 "Consultancy and Advocacy as Radical Anthropology". *Social Analysis* 47(1):116–123.

Janes, Craig 2003 "Criticizing with Impunity? Bridging the Widening Gulf between Academic Discourse and Action Anthropology in Global Health". *Social Analysis* 47(1):90–95.

Jorgensen, Dan 2001 "'Who and What Is a Landowner?' Mythology and Marking the Ground in a Papua New Guinea Mining Project". In Alan Rumsey and James Weiner (eds) *Mining and Indigenous Lifeworlds in Australia and Papua New Guinea*, pp. 68–100. Adelaide: Crawford House Publishing.

Kirsch, Stuart 2001 "Changing Views of Place and Time along the Ok Tedi". In Alan Rumsey and James Weiner (eds) *Mining and Indigenous Lifeworlds in Australia and Papua New Guinea*, pp. 182–207. Adelaide: Crawford House Publishing.

Keen, Ian 1999 "The Scientific Attitude in Applied Anthropology". In S. Toussaint and J. Taylor (eds) *Applied Anthropology in Australasia*, pp. 27–59. Nedlands: University of Western Australia Press.

King, Victor T. 1999 *Anthropology and Development in South-East Asia: Theory and Practice*. Kuala Lumpur: Oxford University Press.

Kressel, Gideon M. 2003 *Let Shepherding Endure: Applied Anthropology and the Preservation of a Cultural Tradition in Israel and the Middle East*. New York: State University of New York Press.

Mars, Gerald 2004 "Refocusing with Applied Anthropology". *Anthropology Today* 20(1):1–2.

Nolan, Riall 2002 *Development Anthropology: Encounters in the Real World*. Boulder: Westview Press.

Peace, Adrian 2003 "Hindmarsh Island and the Politics of Anthropology". *Anthropology Today* 19(5):1–2.

Povinelli, E. 1993 *Labor's Lot: The Power, History, and Culture of Aboriginal Action*. Chicago: University of Chicago Press.

Raz, Aviad E. 2004 *The Gene and the Genie: Tradition, Medicalization, and Genetic Counseling in a Bedouin Community in Israel*. Durham, N.C.: Carolina Academic Press.

Robins, Steven 2003 "Talking in Tongues: Consultants, Anthropologists, and Indigenous Peoples". *Social Analysis* 47(1):121–136.

Rumsey, Alan and James Weiner (eds) 2001 *Mining and Indigenous Lifeworlds in Australia and Papua New Guinea*. Adelaide: Crawford House Publishing.

Sagir, Bill F. 2001 "The Politics of Petroleum Extraction and Royalty Distribution at Lake Kutubu". In Alan Rumsey and James Weiner (eds) *Mining and Indigenous Lifeworlds in Australia and Papua New Guinea*, pp. 145–156. Adelaide: Crawford House Publishing.

Sillitoe, Paul 2000 "Let Them Eat Cake: Indigenous Knowledge, Science, and the 'Poorest of the Poor'". *Anthropology Today* 16(6):3–7.

Sillitoe, Paul, Alan Bicker, and Johan Pottier (eds) 2002 *"Participating in Development": Approaches to Indigenous Knowledge*. ASA Monographs no 39. London and New York: Routledge.

Stewart, Pamela J. and Andrew Strathern 2001a. *Humors and Substances: Ideas of the Body in Papua New Guinea*. Westport, Conn., and London: Bergin and Garvey.

———— 2002 *Remaking the World: Myth, Mining and Ritual Change among the Duna of Papua New Guinea*. Washington, D.C.: Smithsonian Institution Press.

———— 2004 "Indigenous Knowledge Confronts Development among the Duna of Papua New Guinea". In Alan Bicker, Paul Sillitoe and Johan Pottier (eds) *Development and Local*

Knowledge. New Approaches to Issues in Natural Resource Management, Conservation, and Agriculture, pp. 51–63. London and New York: Routledge.

——— (eds) 2001b "Anthropology and Consultancy". Special Issue of *Social Analysis* 45(2).

Stirrat, R. L. 2000 "Cultures of Consultancy". *Critique of Anthropology* 20(1):31–46.

Toussaint, Sandy and Jim Taylor (eds) 1999 *Applied Anthropology in Australasia*. Nedlands: University of Western Australia Press.

Wardlow, Holly 2001 "The Mount Kare Python: Huli Myths and Gendered Fantasies of Agency". In Alan Rumsey and James Weiner (eds) *Mining and Indigenous Lifeworlds in Australia and Papua New Guinea*, pp. 32–67. Adelaide: Crawford House Publishing.

Weiner, James 1999 "Culture in a Sealed Envelope: The Concealment of Aboriginal Heritage and Tradition in the Hindmarsh Island Bridge Affair". *Journal of the Royal Anthropological Institute* 5(2):193–210.

Weiner, James 2001 "Introduction: Depositings". In Alan Rumsey and James Weiner (eds) *Mining and Indigenous Lifeworlds in Australia and Papua New Guinea*), pp. 1–11. Adelaide: Crawford House Publishing.

Willigen, John van 2002 *Applied Anthropology: An Introduction*. 3rd edition. Westport, Conn., and London: Bergin and Garvey.

INTRODUCTION

Anthropology and Consultancy— Ethnographic Dilemmas and Opportunities

Andrew Strathern and Pamela J. Stewart

Background Concerns

The essays that we have collected here speak to many of the dilemmas inherent in anthropological practice today, as well as to the philosophical roots of anthropology itself. What is our position as anthropologists in the worlds that we study, be it those we are indigenous members of or those to which we are outsiders? Do we see ourselves as relatively detached observers or as persons committed to some program of action in relation to the people we study, and how is our study altered by our involvement? Clearly, we do not need to see these alternatives in absolute terms. Each anthropologist may choose a nuanced position along the continuum from detachment to involvement; or may move from one position to another depending on changing circumstances or projects over time. The idea of participant observation, which has been central to anthropological field-work, itself implies a combination of these two opposites of detachment and involvement, which fieldworkers have to balance out for themselves. Fieldworkers must be able to offer something of value to those with whom they work, and the needs or demands of their subjects do not nec-essarily equate or mesh with what the anthropologist is able to offer or feels is appropriate. As more and more trained anthropologists are study-ing their own cultures it becomes sometimes difficult to balance the place-ment of the anthropologist in the community that she/he is studying and to negotiate and disentangle work situations from those involving close kin and/or friends. These considerations show that many of the dilem-mas which anthropologists particularly face in carrying out consultancy

---

References for this section begin on page 22.

work are in fact implicitly faced by all anthropologists, whatever the sponsorship, constraints, or requirements of their study. One main concern is how to recurrently deal with basic questions of the management of reciprocity in historical contexts influenced by differential distributions of social power.

Consultancy work is the contemporary transformation of applied anthropology and inherits some of the particular problems linked to this branch of the discipline. Two quite different problems are frequently found here. One is the opposition that is sometimes made, on the basis of models from other disciplines, between "applied" and "theoretical" studies. The latter are accorded higher prestige. This opposition, however, is somewhat misconceived. If applied work is to be sound, it must incorporate adequate theory to guide its own analyses; and if theoretical work is to be valid, it has to be applicable to "real world" situations about which it theorizes. The second problem has to do with history. "Applied anthropology" as a category term is sometimes associated with European colonialism and regarded as having arisen as an instrument of imperial domination, a "science of colonialism". The debates on this topic are well-worn. Here we may say that this view of anthropological work greatly oversimplified the relationship between particular anthropologists and the controlling powers in the areas where they worked in colonial times; and although the frameworks of thought of anthropologists were of course influenced by the wider presuppositions of their day, many resisted colonial projects rather than supporting them. Goody, for example, has discussed this question for British anthropologists working in Africa prior to the Independence of African states in the 1950s (Goody 1995:7–25), including mention of the Rhodes-Livingstone Institute research workers evaluated also in Ferguson (1999: 27–29). The association itself probably arose from the employment of anthropologists in governmental service. It is interesting to note that F. E. Williams, who was the government anthropologist in Papua from 1922 to 1943, is remembered nowadays as the author of several fundamental ethnographies of Papuan peoples rather than as an instrument of colonial domination over these same peoples. Williams was employed under the auspices of the colonial native welfare fund in Papua, derived from taxation, and his applied interests largely had to do with education. His extraordinary contributions to ethnography (e.g. Williams 1940) must surely have taken up the bulk of his time and energy to produce; and the Papuan government paid for their publication by the Clarendon Press in Oxford. The fact of working for a government does not necessarily mean that the anthropologist becomes simply an instrument of domination, although it may sometimes be the case: everything depends on the governmental context and program itself.

Ideas about the development process generally also continue to change. The theory of modernization, with its assumptions about technology transfer and the inevitable or desired trajectory of societies toward a global norm shaped by capitalism, has been shown to be deficient for explaining and handling the complexities, variations, and contradictions that constitute post-colonial processes of historical change. Anthropologists, economists, sociologists, historians, and political scientists have all been sent "back to the drawing board" by these complexities and have entered into a new phase of empirical, evidence-based studies informed by ideas regarding political ecology and sustainable development. The work of Arturo Escobar and his collaborators on Latin American social movements, and the involvement in these of non-governmental organizations funded from outside, particularly represents critical trends of analysis in this domain of work (Alvarez, Dagnino, and Escobar 1998; Escobar and Alvarez 1992; Schild 1998). In this context anthropologists have come somewhat to the fore through their close, empirical knowledge of the culturally established thought-worlds of the peoples they study, whether these are their own people or others. James Ferguson, for example, has innovatively brought together local field study and an analysis of the wider political and bureaucratic processes that impact and are impacted by development schemes in his studies of LeSotho in Southern Africa, specifically his work on the Thaba-Tseka stock grazing project, and in his research on the Zambian Copperbelt (Ferguson 1994, 1999). Ferguson's work has contributed to the demise of the myth of modernization in which development was seen in terms of a putative transition from an isolated subsistence 'stage' of economy to a 'modern', capitalist market economy; an approach which ignored the existing historical complexities of the situations encountered, as well as the political conflicts generated by development schemes and their unintended social consequences. Ferguson integrates large-scale sociological analysis with representations of the biographic and cultural worlds of the people who are enmeshed in development processes.

The new emphasis in development studies pays much more heed to these cultural worlds, not as hindrances to development as in earlier views, but as possible vital clues to how development plans should be set up; in other words as valid forms of knowledge not just for the past, but for the future also, and as elements that must be incorporated into rather than factored out of a vision for the society. We may refer to this as the indigenous knowledge (IK) movement within development studies. One well-known anthropologist, whose earlier empirical and theoretical work on a Highlands society of Papua New Guinea was influential in shaping the field of New Guinea studies generally, Paul Sillitoe, has successfully applied his data-based methods of enquiry in the field of IK studies (see, for example, Sillitoe 2000; also Antweiler 1998). Promoting IK studies as an integral feature of discussions about development planning is an intrinsically congenial role for anthropologists, although as Sillitoe notes they may have a hard time trying to demonstrate the relevance of their field of observations to development planners themselves. How, for example, are ideas about important concepts, e.g. spirit beings, to be seen as a relevant resource, rather than a hindrance in introducing new types of crops? Part of the solution lies in demonstrating that the people's own approach to knowledge as such is flexible and open-ended and therefore they may be ready to innovate rather than simply resistant to change. Another part of the solution depends on developing a fundamental respect for the people whose lives are being impacted by change and listening to their wishes and concerns before making plans or implementing them.

The peoples of the Pacific, including Papua New Guinea, whom we have studied as anthropologists are all undergoing quite rapid processes of change and are all involved, one way or another, in development schemes that bring them into articulation with global forces. This means that the ways in which we discuss and analyze their lives must grapple intimately and extensively with such processes, thereby problematizing our units of study and our resources for interpreting the information we gather. Consultancy work emerges in this context as a new role for anthropologists, throwing them not just into "participant observation" but into participation as agents and mediators in the processes of change themselves. Indeed this is more generally the situation for any anthropologist setting out to do a study nowadays in arenas also occupied by governmental, company or NGO agencies concerned with development and change. We think that this was also partly the case in earlier times also, but that the terms of discussion have altered in post-colonial contexts to ones in which wider sets of vocally interested parties are involved. One anthropologist whose work we know, for example, was faced with hostilities from an NGO in an African context in ways comparable to those experienced by two of our contributors (Wagner and West) and was eventually forced to leave the field because of this. In another recent instance, relating to work in a Pacific island, the government of an anthropologist's country of origin attempted to coerce the anthropologist into forms of applied work there that were unconnected with the anthropologist's own projected study. In this case, the anthropologist was able to resist these suggestions. When pressure is brought to bear by a national government in an area where a visiting anthropologist from elsewhere is working, such resistance may not be so easy, especially since the visitor depends on national, provincial and local authorities for permission to carry out research of any kind. Conflicts of interest and preference can also arise among the authorities at different levels, or among those at a given level, for example, within the community itself. The arena of research in general, especially in places affected by large-scale development projects, is rather like a minefield through which researchers must pick their way. In more remote areas, less affected by development, this may not be so to the same degree; but all areas reflect in one way or another the contemporary pressures of large-scale change which subtly intertwine themselves with local conflicts and factional or ideological struggles.

As editors of the present collection of essays, our plan was to invite anthropologists who were in various ways involved in these partly new contexts to reflect upon their roles, to stand back from them a little and analyze them, and so to incorporate their own experiences into an unfolding ethnography of change. It is our intention here to provide a forum for individual views and reflections of this kind, building up a portrait of perspectives, rather than developing any programmatic or evaluative views in general. Each contributor therefore presents a personal facet of a complex, emergent situation within our discipline, one that we think is of interest for the problems it raises for every anthropologist, not just those who specifically have done consultancy work as such.

The circumstances and problems our contributors explore are likely to be similar to those that anthropologists have experienced as consultants in other parts of the world. It is by convenience, rather than theoretical design, that the studies presented here belong to Papua New Guinea. What gives them their particular flavor is the mix of post-colonial historical factors that have conditioned the ethnographic work of anthropologists generally in Papua New Guinea in recent years: for example, the combination of people's eagerness for development as such, the democratic processes of government, and the extraordinary opportunities given to companies and to NGOs to pursue their own agendas; along with the severe difficulties of containing violence and resentment of local peoples when they become disillusioned with government or company actions.

There is a further reason why it is apt and timely to produce a set of reflective studies of this kind on Papua New Guinea (PNG) today. This is that there has been an escalation of consulting work done in PNG by professional anthropologists, which may be described as the emergence of a special class of applied anthropological workers who have become quite significant in the overall process of development itself. When we first thought of collecting a set of essays to edit on consultancy work, while visiting at the James Cook University of Northern Queensland in Australia in 1997, we attempted to bring together a number of these anthropologists and to find company, university, or governmental funding, for a workshop where they could discuss their experiences as consultants and how this work affected their placement in anthropology as a whole. We received expressions of interest, but in the end all the anthropologists, lawyers, and others whom we approached were too busy actually doing consultancy work to find one single time to sit down and discuss the topic together. We therefore shifted the venue to the Association for Social Anthropology in Oceania (ASAO) meetings which we describe below, aiming to attract interest from a wider set of professionals.

The growth of consultancy work in Papua New Guinea, particularly in regard to large-scale mining operations, is a phenomenon in itself, and prominent participants in it, such as Colin Filer, have recently provided their own reflections on its purposes, dilemmas, vicissitudes and conflicts, as well as its empirical findings and the ethical questions it raises (Filer 1999). This corpus of work makes it particularly interesting to have also a set of studies that attempt to stand back and take stock of the arena of discussion. The positionality of the ethnographic or social impact consultant is a problem that these practitioners have themselves debated and analyzed among themselves in ways that can be compared with the views of our contributors. The issue of involvement and partisanship emerges as central to the debates, tied in with competing analyses of the effects and meanings of development generally which can be related to the critical work of Escobar and Ferguson we have mentioned earlier (Ferguson 1999). Some authors advocate an activist role of supporting the claims of local peoples in the face of environmental damages caused by mining (see Hyndman 1994, 2001). This is in line with the 'tradition' of anthropologists supporting the viewpoints of the people they specifically work with in the contexts of colonial and post-colonial struggles. Colin Filer and John Burton have both shown how a close-grained ethnographic analysis of the process of negotiation about the outcomes of development can itself help to pinpoint where conflicts arise and performance falls short of prescribed aims (Burton 1999; Filer 1999). In several regards they also show how an understanding of historical processes and their ethnographic study can help in devising programs for the future, particularly with respect to baseline studies prior to the beginning of development projects. A range of viewpoints, moderate, activist, and descriptive, is also supplied in a set of essays edited by Glenn Banks and Chris Ballard on the Ok Tedi gold and copper mine (Banks and Ballard 1997). Much earlier, a holistic and balanced anthropological perspective on the 'cultural impact' of the Ok Tedi project was produced by Fredrik Barth and Unni Wikan in a report to the Institute of Papua New Guinea Studies. Their report predicted many of the deleterious sociocultural results of the mine well before they had occurred (Barth and Wikan 1982). Their work was financed by a grant from the Department of Minerals and Energy and administered through the Institute of Papua New Guinea Studies (see also Filer 1999:95). Another collection of essays has examined the complicated issues of 'compensation for resource development' in PNG, studies that engage crucially with the prolonged social effects of mining on communities, and also with the effects of local peoples on mining projects (Toft 1997; for an overview see the introduction to this volume by A. Strathern and for a discussion of environmental pollution from a local viewpoint see Kirsch's essay in the same volume on the Yonggom people downstream from the mine site). Dan Jorgensen has also written about the problem of determining who is a 'landowner' in contexts of change and in relation to compensation claims from mining companies: problems that have inevitably emerged in both the Ok Tedi and the Porgera areas (Jorgensen 1997).

Filer has, in a number of publications, explained the divisive consequences of large compensation payments (e.g. Filer 1997); and these are compounded by processes of indigenous in-migration around the Porgera gold mine site, as some of the contributors to Filer's 1999 edited volume attest (Banks 1999; Biersack 1999; Bonnell 1999; and see also Imbun 2000). In a more general context, Filer has himself provided a nuanced analysis of the question of positionality in a volume on the anthropology of power, edited by Angela Cheater. Clearly answering to the critical terms of earlier discussions, he suggests that ethnographic inquiry in general into "the political setting of mineral resource development" normally needs to begin by entering into a dialogue with all the stakeholders, and that in these circumstances it (normally again) makes more sense for the anthropologist to act as a mediator or an "honest broker" (Filer 1999: 89) than as a partisan or advocate. He recognizes, however, that there will be circumstances in which anthropologists may be obliged to adopt a more firm position in order to achieve a transfer of power from 'the system' (e.g. the government, or a company) to 'the community' (ibid.). He therefore gives recognition to both activist and moderate stances, according to circumstances. In addition, we may add, if the anthropologist is not specifically employed as a consultant, there is the legitimate possibility of remaining a concerned, but not directly involved, commentator, whose work may in principle be helpful to all sides; although in partisan contexts such a role is also hard to maintain, as ethnographers working 'in the shadows' of development projects must all have experienced. Our contributors have all been in those shadows in one way or another and in this collection they have tried to introduce some light into them.

The essays in this collection themselves emerged, then, in part from two sessions, co-organized by ourselves and Martha Macintyre, held at the 1999 and 2000 meetings of the Association for Social Anthropology in Oceania, in Hilo, Hawai'i, and Vancouver, British Columbia. Our purpose in organizing these sessions was, in the context of Pacific anthropology generally, to bring together anthropologists who had carried out consultancy work, those who were interested in working as consultants, and those who had not worked as consultants but who were interested in the process whereby consultancy work is done or had observed it from the vantage point of their own work. Many ethical and pragmatic issues arise from consultancy work, and persons doing this work outside of anthropology, such as biologists and geologists, also have to reflect upon the research that they are doing for their own investigations versus the work that they are paid to do for companies. They may also have to reflect on their motivations for entering into consultancy work and on whether their own expectations and ambitions have been realized through doing it.

We became interested in the topic in the 1990s when it became evident to us that more people that we spoke with, especially in Australia, were conducting some forms of consultancy work. Often these were people who had been working in a particular area with a set of people for a number of years and had written ethnographic studies in academic contexts.

Companies were now approaching these same persons for their expertise in order to negotiate with local people over a myriad of issues such as land use, water use, labor forces, and compensation payments, and also on how to carry out social impact research (see Goldman 2000).

We were interested to know what the reflections of these people might be on the ways in which the consultancy process impacts ethnographic work and the ethnographer; also, to consider what aims, theories, aspirations and tools the ethnographer brings to the consultancy work itself. A major question is how consultancy impacts ethnographic work and vice-versa. Issues of the kind that concern anthropologists who work in consultancy contexts are bound to emerge during the course of reflecting on the overall process of engagement with consultancy. These issues have to do with the types of development projects that are at stake, the funding of such projects, control over the projects and the results generated by them, relationships between indigenous people and development agencies, and the like. In other words, questions relating to development are tied in directly with questions of values and overall aims and therefore also with the ethical and political situation of the anthropologist. Specific professional matters are also likely to be involved, primarily having to do with rights over materials gathered, freedom to publish, freedom or otherwise to disagree with policy objectives or pragmatic decisions of hiring agencies. There is a whole arena here in which anthropologists have built up knowledge, but it has not been drawn into the mainstream of ethnographic and theoretical discussion. In some instances quite a large proportion of the professionals in anthropology spend considerable effort in consultancy work, sometimes in accordance with institutional requirements placed on them. Recently, professional meetings have included sessions on consultancy issues pertinent to a particular country, such as Australia. Yet there is a sense that consultancy work is unusual and is enclaved away from the supposed mainstream array of topics.

We maintain that a rigid compartmentalization of the work of anthropological consultancy within the discipline as a whole is unrealistic. Theory, analysis, description, and practice need to be related to one another, and the pragmatic problems, the ethical questions, and the imponderabilities of making appropriate theoretical analyses which face the anthropologist as consultant also face the anthropologist as general ethnographer. The question of analysis of material in relation to policy aims is particularly and obviously crucial. What otherwise exists only as an imaginary construct here exists in immediate reality, because what the anthropologist writes may result directly in policy choices that are made. Such a fact in turn must lead the contemporary anthropologist to think very hard about issues of truth, accuracy, and interpretation of data: this at a time in anthropology when various "truths" have been thoroughly relativized as a result of the supposed crisis of representation, the question of indigenous versus outsider perspectives, and the whole theory of the positionality of agents who maintain forms of knowledge: all aspects of what has been called for a decade or more "the crisis of postmodernity" in anthropology.

How the Consultancy Process Impacts Ethnographic Work and Ethnographic Writing

In many instances it appears that when individuals are working with a company and also collecting ethnographic data for their own research it can become confusing to the people what their relationship is with these ethnographers and how much to trust them in light of the fact that what they say might be used subsequently by the company in ways that are unanticipated by the local people. Also, situations arise in which local people feel that the ethnographer should be given information particularly in order to possibly obtain some material rewards from companies in the form of compensation payments. The relationship can therefore be an uneasy one for the ethnographers, who may feel as though they are being placed in the middle of ongoing disputes or issues between a company and local people. But in some ways this is not unlike the sorts of situations that ethnographers find themselves in generally because local people realize that the ethnographer may be able to make their concerns or frustrations known to the outer world and thus may alert government or other agencies to assist in ways such as improving health care, infrastructure, education, etc.

Unlike many ethnographic contexts in which a person or two people go to work with a community of people in a closely established context and the people soon learn that the ethnographer works for a university and is hoping to understand enough of the local people's lifeways to write a description of them for an academic community, consultants are seen as tied to the company for which they are working and this tie is one that the local people realize is to be considered in terms of what information to share or withhold.

In the Duna area where we work in the Southern Highlands of Papua New Guinea the people live near to the Strickland river downstream from the Porgera Joint Venture Gold Mining Company. The company commissioned workers to act as consultants who were employed to collect the origin stories called *malu* among the Duna in order to determine which areas of land were claimed as being owned by which local groups. This information was written down in reports that were presented to the company and used in determining compensation payments that were to be made, as mandated by the Papua New Guinea government, for use of the Strickland river by the mine as a site for the mine's tailings runoff. The knowledge of these *malu* origin stories is owned by members of a group and is exceedingly complex in detail. The particular parts of a *malu* narrative that are given are determined by the context in which the story is being told and what is at stake in the telling of the story. The versions of these *malu* that would have been collected for the water use payments would have highlighted particular points that a telling in another context might not recount in the same way. The basic story line remains the same but particular details are either recounted or not depending on their significance in particular circumstances. Thus, definitive versions of *malu* cannot be obtained, only versions of *malu* that are context dependent. This in turn illustrates the contextual character of what is to be seen as a "true" version of a story. In contexts of this sort one influence may be the expectations of receiving compensation payments. Lorenzo Brutti in his essay for this collection examines in detail this same issue on the basis of his intensive work with the Oksapmin people, western neighbors of the Duna with whom we work.

A more general issue that arises here has to do with rights over materials for publication. Consultants may be required by their sponsors to produce reports only for the sponsors themselves. Negotiations over rights to the wider publication of findings, particularly if these are critical of the sponsoring organizations themselves, may be complicated. Anthropologists to whom we have spoken about this problem report varying experiences. One senior anthropologist indicated that there was indeed a serious problem here and that this would also constitute a constraint in discussing the consultancy role itself. A few younger anthropologists claimed that in their case the company that had hired them would allow them also to use all of their data for their own Ph.D. studies. The situations that emerge are comparable to those of natural scientists who do research paid for by companies and then find that the companies refuse them the rights normally claimed by academics to publish their findings. Close attention to this problem by organizations and individual scientists seems warranted and fundamentally important. The difficulty is that the sponsor and the research worker may have different interests and aims, which can come into conflict. In the absence of third party adjudication being available, it is the research worker who is vulnerable. Here is one arena where professional associations need to expand their concerns for regulations in research to include more fully a concern for the rights of the research workers themselves vis-à-vis sponsors.

Types of Development Projects and Their Relevance for Consultancy Work

The type of development project involved influences greatly the question of how consultancy work can be pursued. There is a great difference between projects designed to help local people themselves to develop small-scale businesses or farming activities, for example, and large-scale mining, logging, or fishing enterprises involving international corporate capital, investment flows, and requirements for profit margins by companies and their shareholders. Anthropologists tend to be involved either in working for government bodies to assist in development work with local communities, or in working for companies to try and improve communication between the company and local communities impacted by development. In both cases their role depends on the knowledge they have, or can acquire, of how local community processes work. In particular, they are often involved in trying to advise on several areas of concern for the development involved.

The first and most fundamental area is that of community representation. What is the community and how is leadership exercised in it? Who can represent its views? Are there factional differences within it? Who holds the rights to various resources that may be at stake? This point corresponds to the second fundamental area, that of rights to resources, including how these are divided up between kinsfolk, and between men and women and older and younger people. Since the resources involved are also those that the company is using or seeking to use, a third area of concern that emerges from the first two areas is that of the distribution of returns to the people from the company's project. Such distribution usually takes the form of a benefits package offered to people in terms of royalties on sales, fees for access rights, land damages payments, transfer of ownership of resources, investment options, or educational, housing, or communications improvements, and the like, the idea being to balance long-term and short-term benefits. From the standpoint of local people in a country such as Papua New Guinea, the whole package is often referred to simply under the rubric of compensation and likened to the payments the people make among themselves for killings or injuries to persons. They place a premium accordingly on large scale single cash payments but are also happy to receive services that extend over time. They see these services as all implicitly a part of the compensation paid to them, and therefore as something the company in fact owes to them. The development process itself impacts local social organization. Given people's preferences for cash payments and immediate distribution of these several further consequences arise. First, the money is dissipated quickly, entering a ramified network of exchanges. Second, disputes arise between people about the equity of distribution. Third, new people become prominent in the community as a result of gaining benefits. And fourth the alignment of groups and factions in the community shifts in accordance with a new power situation.

What we may call spatial and temporal factors are also important. People who live close to a large development arena such as a mine are affected considerably and in many ways within a short period of time. These effects may in turn last for a long time subsequently. While one generation may benefit broadly from company payments, the next generation may feel left out or may want more. In cases where people live on the periphery of influence of a mining enterprise, they are concerned more to contribute at some level to its work force and to obtain spin-off benefits such as a health center or a road or to receive compensation for environmental damages such as river pollution caused by mine tailings. Over time, whether an area is close to or distant from the mine, people's ideas change. Factors such as environmental damage, for instance, may not enter into people's thoughts until a decade or so after a mine is established. At first it is often the case that they are primarily interested in getting a share of cash returns. Later they may become more seriously concerned about the environment, at which point international non-government organizations may also get involved on their behalf. The people far from the mine area usually have little influence over mine policies, but in the long run they may seriously suffer from the mine's indirect environmental effects as well as benefiting from payments and infrastructural improvements.

We cite these rather well-known points in order to highlight how all of the factors involved must inevitably impact the anthropologist as consultant. Good advice at one stage may not be so good at a later stage of a project. Understanding how the community "works" or is changing has continually to be updated. The anthropologist's work is enhanced if it is marked by regular visits and maintained over time. If the involvement is long term, the people may over time come either to blame the anthropologist for 'failures' to influence policy or praise the anthropologist for 'successes' in doing so but expect that these 'successes' can be prolonged and surpassed in the future.

If we compare these longer term processes to the situations of ethnographers outside of consultancy contexts we can see parallels. The longer the fieldwork period, the more people may become dissatisfied with the returns they get from the research worker, for example. When people have become used to getting benefits from a company or other private bodies they may begin to expect from the ethnographer things that only their government or a corporate organization can provide. In a region where some people work as consultants and other research workers are carrying out a different set of inquiries, confusions and difficulties about expectations of returns can arise. These confusions reflect community divisions and factions that already exist and they can also cause new constellations of factions to arise. These same problems affect both consultants and non-consultants as research workers because of the inherently political character of their positions in relation to the communities in which they work. This political position of the research worker can be characterized by the following elements:

1. The research worker is interstitial between power groups.
2. The people may therefore overestimate the research worker's ability to mediate between these groups.
3. The research worker is perceived as someone whose loyalty to one or another interest group must be won.

4. The research worker must then demonstrate this kind of loyalty; but from the researcher's own viewpoint it is most important to be able to preserve a degree of neutrality, in order to remain impartial.

For consultant anthropologists the situation is doubly difficult if they have worked as "mainstream" researchers with the community previously but are now being employed by a company to which they have contractual obligations.

Consultancy versus "Mainstream" Work in Anthropology

Consultancy work is often spoken of in terms apart from "mainstream" or "non-applied" research work. In practice, once people enter into consultancy work, as we have seen earlier, their work does become differentiated, because of the special demands of the consultancy work itself. For example, consultants are more legally accountable to their immediate employers than are anthropologists who work for universities or research institutions. It is worth remembering, however, that professional bodies such as the American Anthropological Association and individual universities in the United States lay down a long list of standards of practice for all research work. At universities an Institutional Review Board, operating in accordance with Federal US principles, approves and monitors all research involving human subjects that is funded from the US itself. However, such constraints do not bear so directly on the "independent" research worker as on the consultant.

The gap between consultancy work and "mainstream" work has recently closed in some ways and widened in others. It has closed somewhat because of the processes usually signified by the term "globalization". Given the spread of education, literacy, and information media throughout the world, what an anthropologist publishes about the people may more quickly be read by the people and in some instances people within research communities are conducting their own anthropological research after receiving higher education degrees. The anthropologist is thus accountable to the people with whom the work is done in a way that parallels the accountability of the consultant anthropologist. This may in particular apply to indigenous anthropologists working in their own communities, and especially if they are employed as consultants there.

On the other hand consultant anthropologists who are contractually employed by companies or governments are, as we have seen, greatly constrained in terms of what they publish and where they publish their results. Here the work that the anthropologist does is less readily available for colleagues at large and thus it is no longer subject to the academic processes of peer review and published debate. Instead it may belong to the agency that hired them. While the work itself may be impartial and may criticize the development project it discusses, its author cannot always publish this criticism elsewhere since to do so might hurt the image and the corporate revenues of their contracting agency. For the consultant anthropologist, then, the major need is to have some flexibility in this regard. In practice this may be hard to achieve. Companies may pay the consultant more in order to obtain rights over the worker's writings. The anthropologist may try to negotiate terms which permit the writing of materials that do not blame the company for mistakes, faults of policy, or deficiencies of practice, but this in turn may reduce the interest value of what the anthropologist has to say about the local people affected by the company work.

The "mainstream" and the consultant anthropologists nowadays face a similar range of problems regarding publication, but they are positioned differently in relation to these problems. The range of problems has to do with:

1. Questions of publication rights
2. Questions of use: who can or who will in practice use what is published and in what ways?
3. Questions of regulation: who will regulate processes 1 and 2?

The consultant anthropologist is constrained and regulated by a particular monetary contract in relation to questions 1 and 2. The mainstream anthropologist is constrained more loosely and has a broader range of venues to publish in, but is clearly accountable both to the people worked with as well as to their own institution and to bodies of professional peers at large. Issues of conscience, ethics, and choice are bound to arise for all. Ethnographers are becoming more and more aware of the implications of work published, especially as more indigenous people become involved in anthropological work themselves. Consultant anthropologists work with contractual constraints but in some ways they may be more free to negotiate directly between local people and companies than can be done by mainstream anthropologists.

For both categories a major issue has to do with the potential exploitation of one's writings as opposed to one's intentions in writing. And both categories are faced with the implications of publishing and distributing in written, available form the fluid flows of oral discourse of cultures that have depended on non-literate communication. The research work itself introduces a new set of factors in the communication process and contributes to changing the character of local knowledge itself.

All anthropologists as fieldworkers and writers are both enclaved in particular contexts and also incorporated into wider spheres of communication. The major problem that distinguishes the consultant's position from that of others has to do with rights of publication and consequences of what is written in terms of immediate impact on local people in regard to compensation and services provided. Until consultants are able to "tell more" about their consultancy work, that work will remain enclaved in special contexts. In many ways the consultancy projects themselves might benefit from a wider input into their research endeavors through receiving the reflections of colleagues at large, because many problems and dilemmas are shared by all anthropologists, as we have argued here.

This Collection of Edited Essays

The essays presented here richly illustrate both the problems and perspectives we have touched on so far and reveal a number of further dimensions of interest. These dimensions arise out of the diversity of contexts that the essays cover under the rubric of consultancy work itself. The first two essays, by Marta Rohatynskyj and Richard Scaglion, portray anthropologists working for governmental agencies, Rohatynskyj at provincial and Scaglion at national level. Rohatynskyj was concerned with "inter-ethnic" relations, Scaglion with "customary law", both classic matters of ethnographic analysis in general in Papua New Guinea (PNG). The second set of essays deals with a phenomenon of growing significance, the activities of non-governmental organizations (NGOs) in development programs. John Wagner worked as an anthropologist in the area of the Kamiali conservation project in Morobe Province, PNG, which, he writes, "was shut down largely as a consequence of villagers' perceptions that their own interests in the project were taking a back seat to those of the facilitating NGO" (Wagner, this volume). In such a context the word "facilitating" reveals a certain irony. In a similar vein, but for a different region, Paige West writes of the Crater Mountain Wildlife Management Area among the Gimi speakers of the Eastern Highlands Province, that the conservation NGO personnel involved in the project developed their own forms of discourse about the people which "facilitated" or legitimized their ideas about how the project was to be controlled. West argues that the NGOs in fact appropriated stereotypes purportedly taken from anthropology itself in order to do this, reinventing the idea of "the primitive" much as was done successively in colonial times and in post-colonial periods where modernization theory held sway (see our previous discussion here). Another irony emerged here, then, for West as the ethnographer trying to make her own account of the Gimi People. These two studies take us a step outside of the consultancy context, showing us ethnographers looking at organizations that in effect operate as consultancies to governments and questioning the ideologies in terms of which these NGOs operate. The two essays fit within our overall framework of examining the relationship between ethnographic work and consultancy work by revealing how two anthropologists not employed as consultants became enmeshed in, and perceived the impact of, NGOs involved in 'development' in the areas where they themselves were working as ethnographers. Wagner and West's experiences in this regard reflect the often interstitial, if not peripheral, position anthropologists occupy in relation to governmental and company activities in the areas where they work. It is often their response to circumstances of this sort that sometimes stimulates research workers to become involved in consultancy work and to try to use their knowledge in a wider context.

Two studies deal with consultancy work for companies. Lorenzo Brutti gives a detailed delineation of his work for a gold mining company in the Strickland area of Sandaun province in PNG. Brutti analyzes both the switch in his position from a student-ethnographer working on his Ph.D. research to a temporary company employee carrying out a survey to the company's specifications, and the actual historical and cultural context of the changes the people were experiencing at the time. He also reports on how he managed to use positively his ethnographic training in order to mediate his new relationship to the people studied, while recognizing the ethical quandaries involved. In her essay, Martha Macintyre, who has carried out long-term consultancy work in more than one area for mining companies, reveals one of the analytical concerns which her work has uncovered: how the interaction between local people and company activities can produce gendered discourses in which men use neo-traditional versions of customary notions to legitimize their own access to company benefits and to place constraints on women's access to these new resources. In both Brutti's study and Macintyre's, then, we see closely observed historical instances of how custom becomes opportunistically reshaped and commodified in the context of development processes; a theme found widespread in the Pacific and elsewhere. The consultancy work brought these themes into high relief in the experiences of the anthropologists themselves.

More and more nowadays, anthropologists are finding themselves involved to one degree or another in consultancy work. Sometimes in fact they do this work for free for companies so as to try to better conditions of the people they work with, sometimes they do the work for free for the people they are working with who ask them to seek special audiences with company personnel

There are obviously ethical concerns involved in conducting both consultancy work and conducting anthropological research. There are also various practical difficulties in consultancy work, as demonstrated in this entire collection of essays. For example, anthropologists may not see eye to eye with the hosts. Governments or companies may place requirements on work that are not agreeable to the investigator. On the positive side, we may also argue that prior academic work can feed in well to consultancy work. The existing expertise of our contributors here undoubtedly informed and enriched their consultancy work. All of our contributors also see consultancy activities as a part of an overall reciprocity between anthropologists and their host communities. This certainly does not mean that all anthropologists should have to do consultancy work if they do not want to undertake this. It does mean that those who undertake it see it at least partly as one way to make returns to a community or to benefit that community or the wider units to which its people belong.

Outside of consultancy anthropologists perhaps increasingly are called on to play collaborative roles. In our field areas, for example, we ourselves are frequently asked in a personal capacity to help people in their relations with government or business, thus being placed in the potential roles of mediators or brokers, roles that we are not always in fact empowered or equipped to play. In the part of the Hagen area of the Western Highlands Province of PNG where we work recent archaeological excavations of the Kuk swamp area following the earlier work by Professor Jack Golson and others, have overlapped with our own field visits in the same area where the archaeological work has been carried out. As a further development, there has been a drive by some researchers to set up this area as a World Heritage site with UNESCO. We have been approached on various sides, informally and on a personal basis without being employed as consultants, to act as mediators, advisors, or negotiators in this whole enterprise. This has happened while we were conducting our own independent research in the same local area among the Kawelka people. Those who approached us were both nationals and expatriates specifically involved in the project. We have tried to respond to these requests, particularly for background advice, without becoming directly involved, since to do so would unduly complicate the picture of "stakeholders" in the issues and would also result in heavy pressures to deliver results far beyond our capacities. The way in which we have mediated the difficulties involved has been to put a good deal of initiative and energy into producing or contributing to academic publications (Stewart and Strathern 1998, 2002; Strathern and Stewart 1998, n.d.). The collection of essays that we edited entitled "Kuk Heritage: Issues and Debates in New Guinea" included essays from several Papua New Guineans working at the PNG National Museum who were involved in the Kuk project at one level or another as well as contributions from others who had been working in the Kuk area or had an interest in the Kuk project. We have also, at the request of one of the land-holders, re-written and re-illustrated a version of his own life-history along with other ethnohistorical texts and a set of historical discussions of their wider context, also as a way of providing further information on the area. Our effort has therefore been directed toward making a return in an arena where we are independently working as opposed to involvement in arenas where we are not since we have not been employed in any capacity by those involved (Strathern and Stewart 2000).

Given the sense of an ethical imperative with regard to reciprocity, some anthropologists who have specifically switched to consultancy work have also experienced difficulties, contradictions, and ambivalences in relation to this work. These difficulties have challenged the anthropologists in some cases productively to work through the analytical problems at issue in relation to the terms of reference set for them by sponsors. Marta Rohatynskyj, for instance, was required to investigate "minor ethnic groups" in relation to the dominant group of the Tolai in East New Britain Province in PNG. This formulation stimulated her to rethink the concept of ethnicity involved. Couching her remarks in the language of George Marcus, she writes: "In my struggle to fulfill the terms of reference to the satisfaction of the sponsors, I was forced to confront the limitations of a realist ethnography based on primordial identities, in favor of a multi-locale perspective amenable to a modernist treatment." She came to see the problem along the situational, historical lines advocated by many scholars working on ethnicity today (e.g. Eriksen 1993). In practical terms, a certain ambivalence remained. Treating the people studied, the Baining, as a minority group might give them an advantageous special status, but it could also, she saw, rob them "of the generally held rights of other citizens". In attempting to forestall this possible result she recommended a policy approach based on an inclusive category of "citizens of the province". Rohatynskyj's narrative of her problems and reflections on them turns into an illuminating retrospective on history and on the anthropologist's ongoing roles within history; on the need to move with the times and to both relativize and respect the essentialisms that people throw out in a strategic search for identity.

Richard Scaglion's essay shows us another impressive effort to mediate, in this instance between his new role as a government bureaucratic officer and his earlier one as an "independent" anthropologist in the field. Scaglion had the important job of fashioning a program of research on customary law to support the move toward Village Courts in PNG after Independence came in 1975. He was in charge of a team of local research workers, whom he also had to train for their tasks. He had the opportunity to apply his own "modernist" view of customary law; that is, to stress the importance of "procedural law—the processes by which disputes were actually resolved—rather than substantive law—the 'rules' that most Melanesians seemed to lack but that the lawyers seemed to think were so important". Scaglion was thus placed as an anthropologist among lawyers in the capital city of Port Moresby, while to the village people he studied he became an important point of possible access to the power and wealth of the capital, a patron-figure instead of being simply a friend. He was faced with the objectifying practices of both his colleagues in the Law Reform Commission and, in the longer run, villagers themselves in PNG who, when confronted with questions about their customs and the legal recognition of these, tend to re-essentialize themselves in order to acquire standing in a new bureaucratic and political world of identities: much as Rohatynskyj found in East New Britain. Scaglion found in general that his post brought with it many pressures he had not experienced before. He became annoyed with fellow-anthropologists who were better at pointing out problems than coming up with solutions (a complaint that colonial government officers frequently used to make in general, questioning what was the use of anthropological information for their purposes). Scaglion had to deal with demands for policy solutions, and he found himself at times in disagreement with draft legislation the Commission was proposing, for example, against the practice of "excessive compensation" payments for offenses. In regard to this issue he took the tack we also later took in relation to the Kuk heritage issues: he pulled together and edited a volume of contributions in which anthropologists argued that making too rigid a set of rules would stifle the adaptive dynamism of indigenous processes of settlement. The bill was accordingly modified. The issue, incidentally, continues, now often transmogrified into claims against the State of Papua New Guinea by local groups (see Stewart and Strathern 1998). Like Rohatynskyj's study, Scaglion's account is both a narrative of an interesting set of role changes and itself an analysis of historical changes at national and local levels in PNG. Their essays amply show, as do the others, that an auto-ethnography of consultancy leads outward into the world of anthropology and history in general.

The two essays by Wagner and West constitute a kind of Intermezzo. They follow a different pathway or theme, playing like a melody that intersects with another. They also, in so doing, reveal a new arena of ethnography, the ethnography of the NGO. It is a narrative, again in modernist vein. NGOs have entered the scene in PNG and elsewhere to provide enlightened action on behalf of local communities in post-colonial contexts. Their workers genuinely profess to assist local people to attain their goals. At the same time they are organizations with their own imperatives, one of which is to obtain funding. Like churches seeking funds from congregations back home for their activities, they set up a discourse of fund-raising that depends on a certain stereotyping of the people they work with. In an acutely observed and argued essay, Paige West draws attention to this discursive practice and shows how it ran counter to her own ways of perceiving and studying the Gimi. Interestingly, perhaps inevitably, her study also turns on a question of identity. The conservationist NGO in her area was committed to a view that Gimi identity was or should be rooted in a primordial past and that contemporary people who no longer practiced the old customs were "not Gimi". West situates her own work and approach in the focus on connections between local sites and global processes, to which, again, Marcus and Fischer have contributed (Marcus 1998; Marcus and Fischer 1999). She therefore expected to look at awkwardly competing representations of the kind she actually encountered. She does not relativize these observations, however; instead she analyzes the NGO's production of stereotypes as one that misrepresents the people. She recognizes that this made her work unpopular with the NGO's workers themselves. Her implication is perhaps that for consultants there is always the danger of adopting or falling into such motivated forms of stereotyping. And yet the people themselves often, at a certain point, self-objectify in similar ways, making their own stereotypes in order to advance their own interests. West poses a difficult question. Can we write in ways that both counter other discursive productions and at the same time avoid deconstructing the people we write about "to the point of powerlessness?"

John Wagner's study is a sharply etched account of the actual historical trajectory of an NGO and of why its efforts failed. Wagner's argument in many ways follows on from that of West, pursuing it further into the realm of praxis. He asks why the Kamiali conservation project was shut down, and answers that it was not grounded well enough in the actual institutions of local communities. In other words, incomplete ethnography can have real-world results in the context of development activities. This reinforces the point of the importance that anthropologists feel attaches to their own work as consultants. Wagner also stresses that conservation projects make biodiversity a kind of resource in itself, to which they claim custodial rights. This again sets up a problem of control and participation. The local people are unlikely to see the matter in the way the NGO personnel do. They may see NGO personnel as acting in a self-interested way, even though these personnel say they are there only to help the villagers. The parallel with perceptions of colonial officials is clear. For consultancy work this is another cautionary tale. It would be interesting to know what responses NGOs would make to these ethnographic accounts of their work. Surely some anthropologists have worked as consultants for NGOs and will know the issues from that perspective.

The case of the NGOs bridges over from that of government to the case of consultancy for companies, organizations explicitly and clearly, rather than implicitly or ambiguously as in the case of NGOs, set up to benefit themselves. Lorenzo Brutti provides a detailed ethnography of his work for the Porgera Joint Venture company (PJV). The setting is fairly benign, for his task was to gather basic ethnographic data to determine how payments should be made to local people for the use of the Strickland river in PNG as a means of waste-disposal by PJV. PJV sponsored and paid for the study, but it was obviously in everyone's interests to see that the study was carried out accurately. On the other hand, the prospect of payment must have influenced people's narratives and it certainly led to demands for payments that would be adequate to share among numerous groups, as it did among the neighboring Duna people (see Stewart and Strathern 2002). Brutti was therefore in the thick of a local political situation and experienced its pressures accordingly. His position here paralleled to some degree that of Scaglion, although he was not a government bureaucrat. As an ethnographer, he felt he needed to explain to the company the "eco-cosmological" reasons why the water-use permit payments were very important. The study probably sharpened his knowledge of this cosmology and thus contributed to the deepening of his ethnographic knowledge. Among the Duna we ourselves observed in 1999 an efflorescence of "myth-related" narratives and recitations of origin stories of groups that occurred in the context of a company drilling for oil at the Strickland river area (Stewart and Strathern 2002). Brutti further proposed ways in which the company should follow up the payments for water-use. Here he adopted an ethical role on behalf of the people, going beyond the remit of his sponsored study. We see him stepping back into the shoes of the anthropologist as local advocate. But he also acknowledges that the people saw him differently, and stepping back and forth between roles may not be so easy.

Brutti's meticulous study and his ethical concerns are matched by Martha Macintyre's essay on gender relations and development in the context of mining. Her findings resonate with the theme of self-objectification we have found in some of the other essays. In a powerfully argued presentation, she notes that men can be inventive in finding "customary" reasons why women should not share equally in job opportunities and benefits of development. Again, we find that consultancy work has pitched the anthropologist into a valuable but painful arena of observations, enriching the ethnographic experience and placing it into the heart of struggles for power. She writes, "While academics delight in the diversity and hybridity of Melanesian religious cults and practices, noting the imaginative blend of western, traditional, and global elements, communities struggle with the social disruption and internal conflicts they generate". As consultants, anthropologists are drawn into the core of such conflicts. As fieldworkers they are also brought close to them. These encounters touch on an overlapping range of issues, dilemmas, and opportunities which Macintyre energetically explores.

We are happy to present these contributions to what we think is an important topic, the contested arena of anthropology and consultancy; not because we regard consultancy as a special domain of enquiry, different from others, but rather for the reverse reason, that issues which emerge through consultancy work speak in an urgent way to issues in anthropology at large. Equally, we think the studies presented here show that consultancy work and commentaries on it must be looked at in the light of anthropological theory and practice as a whole.

Acknowledgments

We wish to thank all of those present at the ASAO sessions, both in the audience and in the panels, who provided us with insights into the topic and thoughtful comments. We thank John Young in particular in this regard for his useful observations based on his successful long-term career work in the field of consultancy and ethnography, and his suggestions of ways in which consultancy can involve good ethnography. A part of this Introduction was also presented jointly by us as invited speakers to the 'Japan Society for International Development' on May 13, 2000, at Waseda

University in Tokyo, Japan. We thank Dr. Hironari Narita for inviting us and hosting us on that occasion. We also thank all those who commented on our presentation at the time. Further, we wish to thank the anonymous reviewers of this collection for many helpful comments and suggestions on all the essays, and to Michael Lambek and Janice Boddy for their support of the project as a whole.

References

Alvarez, Sonia E., Evelina Dagnino, and Arturo Escobar (eds) 1998 *Cultures of Politics, Politics of Cultures*. Boulder: Westview Press.

Antweiler, Christopher 1998 "Local Knowledge and Local Knowing: An Anthropological Analysis of Contested 'Cultural Products' in the Context of Development". *Anthropos* 93:469–494.

Banks, Glenn 1999 "The Economic Impact of the Mine". In C. Filer (ed) *Dilemmas of Development*, pp. 88–127. (Chapters 3, 6, and 7 in this volume are also by Banks.)

Banks, Glenn and Chris Ballard (eds) 1997 *The Ok-Tedi Settlement: Issues, Outcomes and Implications*. Canberra: Australian National University (Pacific Policy Paper no. 27).

Barth, Fredrik and Unni Wikan 1982 "Cultural Impact of the Ok Tedi Project: Final Report". Boroko: Institute of Papua New Guinea Studies.

Biersack, Aletta 1999 "Porgera—Whence and Whither?" In C. Filer (ed) *Dilemmas of Development*, pp. 260–279.

Bonnell, Susanne 1999 "The Landowner Relocation Programme". In C. Filer (ed) *Dilemmas of Development*, pp. 128–159. (Chapter 2 in this volume is also by Bonnell.)

Burton, John 1999 "Evidence of the 'New Competencies'?" In C. Filer (ed) *Dilemmas of Development*, pp. 280–301.

Eriksen, Thomas Hylland 1993 *Ethnicity and Nationalism: Anthropological Perspectives*. London and Chicago: Pluto Press.

Escobar, Arturo and Sonia E. Alvarez (eds) 1992 *The Making of Social Movements in Latin America: Identity, Strategy, and Democracy*. Boulder: Westview Press.

Ferguson, James 1994 *The Anti-Politics Machine: Development, Depoliticization, and Bureaucratic Power in Lesotho*. Minneapolis: University of Minnesota Press.

Ferguson, James 1999 *Expectations of Modernity: Myths and Meanings of Urban Life on the Zambian Copperbelt*. Berkeley: University of California Press.

Filer, Colin 1999 "The Dialectics of Negation and Negotiation in the Anthropology of Mineral Resource Development in Papua New Guinea". In A. Cheater (ed) *The Anthropology of Power: Empowerment and Disempowerment in Changing Structures*, pp. 88–102. London and New York: Routledge.

——— (ed) 1999 *Dilemmas of Development: The Social and Economic Impact of the Porgera Gold Mine 1989–1994*. Port Moresby: The National Research Institute, and The Australian National University, Canberra.

Goldman, Laurence 2000 *Social Impact Analysis: An Applied Anthropology Manual*. New York: New York University Press.

Goody, Jack 1995 *The Expansive Moment: Anthropology in Britain and Africa 1918–1970*. Cambridge: Cambridge University Press.

Hyndman, David 1994 *Ancestral Rain Forests and the Mountain of Gold: Indigenous Peoples and Mining in New Guinea*. Boulder: Westview Press.

——— 2001 "Academic Responsibilities and Representation of the Ok Tedi Crisis in Postcolonial Papua New Guinea". *The Contemporary Pacific* 13(1):33–54.

Imbun, Benedict Y. 2000 "Mining Workers or 'Opportunist Tribesmen'? A Tribal Workforce in a Papua New Guinea Mine". *Oceania* 71:129–149.

Jorgensen, Dan 1997 "Who and What Is a Landowner? Mythology and Marking the Ground in a Papua New Guinea Mining Project". *Anthropological Forum* 7:599– 628.

Marcus, George E. 1998 *Ethnography through Thick and Thin.* Princeton: Princeton University Press.

Marcus, George E. and Michael M.J. Fischer 1999 *Anthropology as Cultural Critique: An Experimental Moment in the Human Sciences.* (1st ed. 1986). Chicago and London: The University of Chicago Press.

Schild, Veronica 1998 "New Subjects of Rights? Women's Movements and the Construction of Citizenship in the 'New Democracies'". In S.E. Alvarez et al. (eds) *Cultures of Politics, Politics of Cultures,* pp. 93–117. Boulder: Westview Press.

Sillitoe, Paul 2000 "Let Them Eat Cake: Indigenous Knowledge, Science and the 'Poorest of the Poor'". *Anthropology Today* 16(6):3–7.

Stewart, Pamela J. and Andrew Strathern 1998 "Money, Politics, and Persons in Papua New Guinea". *Social Analysis* 42(2):132–149.

Stewart, Pamela J. and Andrew Strathern 2002 *Remaking the World.* Washington, D.C.: Smithsonian Institution Press.

Strathern, Andrew and Pamela J. Stewart 2000 *Stories, Strength, and Self-Narration: Western Highlands, Papua New Guinea.* Adelaide, Australia: Crawford House Publications.

——— n.d. "Hagen Settlement Histories: Dispersals and Consolidations". In P. Swadling, J. Golson, and J. Muke (eds) *Nine Thousand Years of Gardening: Kuk and the Archaeology of Agriculture in Papua New Guinea.* Adelaide, Australia: Crawford House Publications.

——— (eds) 1998 *Kuk Heritage: Issues and Debates in Papua New Guinea.* Pittsburgh: Department of Anthropology, University of Pittsburgh.

Toft, Susan (ed) 1997 *Compensation for Resource Development in Papua New Guinea.* Port Moresby: Law Reform Commission of Papua New Guinea in conjunction with the Australian National University, Canberra.

Williams, Francis E. 1940 *Drama of Orokolo: The Social and Ceremonial Life of the Elema.* Oxford: Clarendon Press.

Chapter 1

ON KNOWING THE BAINING AND OTHER MINOR ETHNIC GROUPS OF EAST NEW BRITAIN

Marta A. Rohatynskyj

Introduction

The question that I was asked to investigate by the Tolai-dominated East New Britain Provincial government was very simply if there was a relationship between the relative underdevelopment of the minor ethnic groups of the province, generally defined as all non-Tolai groups, and their culture. This was the germ of the formulation presented to me when I commenced my duties as a research officer in the Department of Planning and Technical Services within the administrative structure of the Department of East New Britain in 1991. The discussions that followed, in order to operationalize the concepts of this original formulation, I remember as intense, theoretically challenging and forcing me to strategize within an applied context that had few precedents and, it seemed to me, contained many potential pitfalls for the consulting anthropologist. However, I may be overstating the uniqueness of my position. It is clear from the literature that all consultancy or applied work necessitates a relativizing of both the orientation of the sponsor as well as that of the subject population. The anthropologist is in the position of a mediator or cultural broker bearing the full brunt of the ethical responsibility for her recommendations for action. However, I am still struck by the curiosity of the situation: an anthropologist being asked by the dominant ethnic group of the province to account for the shortcomings of all the others, in a word, find out what prevented them from attaining the same level of development as the Tolai themselves.

The factors that contributed to this stance on the part of the Tolai evolved out of the complex colonial history of the province and reflect the degree to which class formation has underpinned the deployment of life-style and cultural identities. The ability of the senior civil servants, who made up the research committee which oversaw my work, to formulate the problem in terms of culture reflects the anthropological sophistication of these men and the degree to which our discipline has contributed to the understanding of educated Papua New Guineans of themselves. This has been accomplished, at least in part, by the work of a number of respected anthropologists in teaching at the University of Papua New Guinea, of which many Tolai senior civil servants are graduates, as well as the fre-quency of interaction of the educated class of Papua New Guineans with researchers and social scientists of various types both at home and abroad.

> It was in the spirit of the common pursuit of a solution to a challenging prob-lem that I presented to them the findings on which I based my recommenda-tions for action. As I will explain more fully in a later section, a major part of the motivation for the commissioning of the study grew out of Tolai concern with rising Baining militancy. In several ways, the study was entangled with various formulations of the 'Baining problem' and thus Tolai/Baining relations were a major focus in my final report. In the report I conclude that at the core of the 'Baining problem' was the nature of the relationship between these two groups and not a failing of the Baining: "The particular history of Baining/Tolai inter-action has resulted in a rigid ethnic boundary with exaggerated values ascribed to each ethnic identity. This I have argued has resulted in an element of racial-ism as characteristic of the relationship, particularly in the Baining internaliza-tion of the negative evaluation". (Rohatynskyj 1992:132)

Klaus Neumann, who had carried out extensive historical research with various Tolai communities, commented upon reading the report that pre-senting it to Tolai government officials required some courage (pers.com.). In fact, the report was the product of a complex process of negotiation, both explicit and implicit, between me and various government officials which allowed for the development of a common discourse. In a sense, the report itself is an ethnography of non-Tolai groups written in terms generated by my ethnography of Tolai official thinking and government practices. It is tailored to the parameters of a particular Tolai world view more so than to an objectively apprehended reality independent of the inter-subjective understandings developed in the course of the project (Fabian 1994).

The research report I presented to the government is a special case of the 'ethnographic artifact' Sjoerd Jaarsma and I have written about (Rohatyn-skyj and Jaarsma 2000). In our formulation of the concept, we argue that ethnography is shaped by a triad of relationships whose analysis can act as the basis for understanding the particular character of ethnography generated for a specific group at a specific time. Like the ethnographic monograph or journal article, which is formed in the complex relation-ships between the host community, the researcher and the audience of the ethnography, the consultant's report is generated through a similar process. The difference is that the audience brackets the process dictating the terms of the research as well as acting as a final and restricted receptor of the text. Academic ethnographic texts are shaped by the conventions of the discipline as communicated to the author through the social processes of training, various peer review fora and the requirements of publication. The parameters of the consultant's report are set by the terms of reference of the research agreed to by the contractor and researcher as well as the author's appreciation of the terms in which results will most readily be accepted. Because the audience overtly sets the parameters for the text directly prior to the commencement of research, often restricting possible directions quite categorically, the relationship between the audience and the researcher becomes more emphasized than the one between the researcher and the community of study in the formulation of the text of the resulting report. This is so, in the sense that concern with meeting the requirements of the audience takes precedence in the shaping of the text. However, it does not mean that ethical considerations or obligations to the host community are diminished. Indeed, in phrasing my conclusions in the language that I did, I was presenting an artifact specifically crafted to the sensibilities of the contractors as well as serving the interests of the minor ethnic groups of East New Britain, as I saw them at the time.

In discussing the changes that have occurred in ethnography as a result of globalization, Jaarsma and I underlined the degree to which the ethnographic subjects of ethnography now compose the audience for ethnography (Rohatynskyj and Jaarsma 2000:11). This consultancy experience could be seen as unique in that the sponsors of the research are both traditional and contemporary subjects of ethnography. Here then is a further blurring of the boundaries between the three positions outlined in our schema of the generation of ethnographic texts: the researcher, the audience and the native. What is unique and intriguing about the particular situation that I found myself in was that I had to negotiate not just my stance in relation to one group's assertions of uniqueness but those of at least two groups who saw themselves as historically linked and opposed. The blurring of boundaries between the elements acting to generate ethnography as well as the consultancy context which placed me literally between two group interests, I will argue, demanded a modernist approach to ethnography as opposed to a realist one, in the sense that ethical concerns growing out of mutually entailing comparisons come to the forefront.[1] As Marcus (1994:327–328) writes:

> But while modernist ethnography operates fully cognizant of the history of the political and economic circumstances in which identities have been formed, it is not built explicitly around the trope of power, but rather of ethics, that is, the complex moral relationship of the observer to the observed, of the relevance of the observed's situation to the situation of the observer's own society, and

ultimately the exploration of the critical purpose of contemporary ethnographic analysis.

In this essay, I would like to compose another layer of ethnography over this consultancy experience, evaluating the interplay between these overlapping positions and frameworks. I will document the perspectives of the sponsors and the consultant and their negotiation of a common discourse manifested in the final research report. Of particular interest in this process is the development of an appreciation of what it meant both to Tolai and others in the context of the political and economic realities of East New Britain in the early 1990s to be a 'successful ethnic group'. It is this concept which bridges the various levels and foci of ethnography discussed and is clearly anchored in my research concerns both before and after the consultancy experience. In addressing these issues the similarities between the knowledge generated by traditional, academic ethnographic research and the consultancy experience will be considered. I will argue that the premises of the traditional ethnographic approach as opposed to those of the consultancy experience place the researcher in distinct positions whose perspectives constrain the nature of analysis. The perspective that I developed in completing this particular study forced me to appreciate in a very fundamental way the requirements of a modernist as opposed to a realist ethnography and to understand the two stances as legitimate responses to different sociopolitical contexts and goals.

The Background to the Research Project

The Province of East New Britain forms roughly the eastern half of the island of New Britain. One of the first provinces to be established upon national independence in 1975, its population in the 1990 national census was recorded as just under 200,000.[2] Two-thirds of this population was concentrated in the Gazelle Peninsula, where the Tolai were dominant but coexisted with a mixed population of Papua New Guineans both from within and outside of the island. As well, small populations of non-Papua New Guineans resided on the Gazelle reflecting the complex history of the Rabaul/Kokopo area as an administrative and commercial center dating from the German colonial era. One-third of the population was spread over the vast areas referred to as the Baining, the mountainous hinterland of the Gazelle, and the Pomio region, referring to the southwestern balance of provincial territory. The history of Tolai ascendancy to their dominant position on the national scene as a well-educated, and politically and economically engaged, population highly integrated into the metropolitan culture of the country forms a fascinating aspect of Papua New Guinean national history. Tellingly, Errington and Gewertz (1995) document the degree to which Tolai symbols of identity vied in the early 1990s for the position of national identity symbols. In modern ethnography, the Tolai have been positively treated in relation to European values and much is made of their distinctiveness in relation to other Papua New Guinean peoples both in their early assimilation of European skills and in their penchant for capitalism (A.L. Epstein 1969; T.S. Epstein 1968; Salisbury 1970). Many writers note the importance of the persistence of *tabu*, traditional shell money, in both facilitating and representing Tolai uniqueness (A.L. Epstein 1979). Neumann (1992) links Tolai cultural assurance to the history of modifications and adaptations of traditional customs to contemporary settings contrasting them with other neighboring groups who suffered loss of traditional practices and symbols of identity and then struggled to revive them. A.L. Epstein (1999:48–50) documents the degree to which the Tolai sense of uniqueness in relation to non-Tolai resulted in a sense of superiority if not an arrogance.

The specific set of events that precipitated the Tolai-dominated provincial government to engage an anthropologist to investigate the larger problem of ethnic identity and economic development of the minor ethnic groups, grew out of the possibility of the installation of a gold mine on Baining traditional land in the Sinivit Community Government Area.[3] As early as 1986, a consultant had been engaged to carry out land demarcation in the Wild Dog prospecting area. This process, along with long-held resentments against Tolai encroachments on Baining land, resulted in the formation of the Masi Welfare Association. The association was founded by educated members of the Mali and Simbali linguistic groups, the most southern and smallest linguistic divisions of the Baining, thus the name. Although it arose in response to the practicalities of accommodating a major resource extraction project and the need to determine legal claim, the association at one time, according to informants, enjoyed the support of all five of the Baining groups ranging from the base of the Gazelle Peninsula at Wide Bay to its north easternmost tip at Cape Lambert.

In preparation for my research, I was given access to correspondence and records documenting discussions between the association and the provincial government. There are a number of issues identified. Although the possibility of the Wild Dog Mine precipitated the formation of the association, the larger concern of fair and equitable land administration emerges as a major problem in the correspondence. Association members were worried about the future establishment of settlement schemes on Baining territory; while the government worried about the restructuring of the relationship between the National Lands Unit and the Provincial Lands Division in order to provide adequate service. Given the high population density of the Tolai-dominated local government areas, Baining fears of future encroachment by Tolai were well founded. The Baining account of Baining/Tolai relations hinges on a Baining retreat from the fertile areas of the coast before the invading Tolai. In many ways the Baining saw themselves as a conquered people both by the Tolai and the colonial governments. The historic confiscation of large tracts of land by the Catholic Mission for plantation use, was justified by the administration of the time as recompense for the St. Paul's Massacre of 1904, when Baining murdered a group of Catholic missionary priests, brothers and nuns (Hempenstall 1978; Rohatynskyj 2000).

Although land was a prime concern, the language of the Masi Welfare Association soon turned to the question of their ability to participate in the decision making processes of development efforts and to the integrity of their ethnic identity. I have among my papers an agenda of a meeting between government representatives and the Masi Welfare Association held in 1989 whose topic was 'Protection of Baining Land, Culture and Ethnic Identity'. One of the items listed for discussion is the creation of a Ministry of Minor Ethnic Groups. The item appears to be supported by a letter from an association member, so it is reasonable to assume that this proposal was a Baining initiative. In 1990 the premier of the province, the Honorable Sinai Brown, produced a discussion paper on the establishment of an Office of Ethnic and Cultural Affairs and a senior research officer in the Department of Planning and Technical Services was appointed to produce a situation report on the Baining. The initial terms of reference were aimed very much at establishing population, geographical location, language and cultural practices of the Baining. A second concern was the Masi Welfare Association and the range of political involvement of the community with institutions outside the Baining area. Finally, the question of the level of development of the Baining in relation to the Mengen, who dominate the Pomio area, and the Tolai was raised.

It is interesting that in his position paper, the Premier makes reference to the preamble of the provincial constitution, which does not name the multitude of ethnic groups traditionally resident in the province. In fact the constitution only makes reference to five geographical areas: the Bainings, Duke of York Islands, Gazelle Peninsula, Pomio and Watom Island (East New Britain Provincial Government 1977:9). However, in declaring the second goal of the government as 'all citizens to have an equal opportunity to participate in, and benefit from, the development of our province', universal literacy in Pisin, Kuanua (the language of the Tolai), Mengen or English and in *tokples* is seen as instrumental. Although in this document the question of the multitude of traditionally constituted ethnic groups was not directly confronted, concern with the concept of ethnicity in relation to culture and political representation could be seen as at the core of perceived forms of appropriate political organization and democracy by the provincial administration.

It is not difficult to find a parallel between the efforts of the Baining to assert themselves against the dominant Tolai with Tolai efforts some twenty years earlier to counteract the control of the Australian government. Indeed, some see the Tolai struggle as itself precipitating national independence (Grosart 1982). Secondly, in 1991, while I was actually conducting my research, Tolai and Baining reacted in a similar way to threats of exposure of their cultural secrets to disrespectful strangers, with Tolai removing a *duk duk* mask from public view (Post-Courier 1991). In parallel fashion, Baining successfully protested the decision of the East New Britain Tourist Board to send their 'fire dancers' to a trade show in Japan and to schedule them as performers at the up-coming South Pacific games. The depth of feeling against these threats to cultural integrity is passionately expressed in a letter by Mr. Boniface Setavo, a Baining leader, to the Editor of the *Post-Courier* dated May 1, 1991. Copies of the letter were sent to the Provincial Minister of Culture and Tourism, the East New Britain Tourism Board, Mr. Henry Saminga, Member of Provincial Assembly for Lasul Baining (the only Baining to sit in the ENB House of Assembly), the Masi Welfare Association and Radio Rabaul. I will quote from an unpublished version of the letter in my possession. The concluding section of the letter is an appeal to a Baining sense of primordial common identity.

> I ask my fellow Bainings to support me. But I shall be disheartened and defeated if my fellow Bainings remain silent. I shall develop a dislike for those politicians concerned in the present Provincial Government and the ENB Tourism Board if they exercise their iron fists and pursue their plans to send the dancers to Japan or even to Port Moresby and Lae during the coming South Pacific Games. I would like to let it be known that encouraging the Bainings to perform their sacred fire dance in such alienated and unnatural surroundings is a show of disrespect and total disregard for the rights and identity of the Bainings and their culture. Yes, it may be good for the tourism industry. Tell me what direct long-term benefits will these trips outside of East New Britain have on the Baining villager?
>
> Long Live my Bainings' sacred fire dance. Kill it and you kill my faith, my hope, life and joy and deep relationship with godly spirits.
>
> It was this deep relationship that my forefathers took years to create and nourished it for me.

It seems to me that this rhetoric could not help but arouse the sympathy of Tolai, as well as any other Papua New Guineans with any sentiment of attachment to ancestral land and spirits.

As much as the parallelism between Baining aspirations to cultural integrity and meaningful development resonated with Tolai contemporary and historical concerns, there was also another element which predisposed the government to a serious consideration of the plight of the Baining and other minor ethnic groups. The work of Klaus Neumann made a deep impact on Tolai understandings of themselves and of ethnicity in general in Papua New Guinea. Neumann had conducted research in the late 1980s in communities close to Rabaul (Neumann 1992). He had formed many deep attachments with various families and individuals and was in close contact with various prominent Tolai. He maintained these ties over the years. Significantly, it was Neumann who was asked to compile an account of the volcanic eruptions which devastated the Rabaul area starting in September 1994 (Neumann 1996). I heard about a talk he had given to senior government officials during the course of my research. One of the ideas that was apparently developed in this talk was the degree to which an acknowledgement of a peoples' history was necessary to the progress of the group. In a sense this educated Tolai community was both ready to claim its own history as well as to investigate the impact that historical forces had had on the inability of the Baining to progress. This particular appreciation of history played a major role in the acceptance of my findings by the government. Further, the Premier, himself, had spearheaded the initiative which resulted in the research I undertook, and he did so out of a deep personal concern for the Baining people. He emphasized that he could trace his descent, at least in part, to the Butam ethnic group which was now extinct. This Papuan language group was said to have been annihilated in the struggle of Tolai and Baining over land in the central Gazelle. Claiming thus a partial kinship with Papuan language speakers in the province which included the Baining, he explained to me that his father had been a Methodist pastor stationed in a Baining area and he, himself, had grown up with a group of Baining friends. His friendship with the Baining boys was close and unfettered by their ethnic and economic differences until the cohort entered primary school. Over the first few years, the Baining boys dropped out, one by one, until there were none left, while he and the other Tolai boys continued. He told me that he had always felt dismayed that close childhood friendships were destroyed by factors he could not quite understand at the time.

Finally, I think there was nostalgia on the part of some senior officials for a simpler time than the one they had to confront in the early 1990s, which predisposed them to a sympathy with the Baining. Contemporary Tolai, although successful in terms of the values of the metropolitan culture of Papua New Guinea, were faced with the problems associated with a sprawling peri-urban area around Rabaul. Crime rates were increasing. The squatter settlements posed a host of problems to local and provincial officials concerned with order and prosperity. Increasingly, Tolai youth appeared to be drifting away from the expectations of their parents, caught up in consumerism, drinking and petty crime.

This appreciation of the context that inspired the Provincial Government to commission such a study is very much a *post facto* phenomenon. It is an appreciation I gained as a result of completing the research and being able to reflect on it for some years afterwards. When I undertook my responsibilities as research officer in February 1991, I had a limited comprehension of the situation I was entering. Ethnographic knowledge, in this case whether of the minor ethnic groups or of the world view of Tolai senior servants, is hard won knowledge, gained through constantly propelling one's social persona to the limits of competence. This total venturing of self, of challenging one's own limitations perhaps can be seen as preserving for participant-observation methodology some of the authority denied it by those skeptical of the value of just 'being there'. By the end of May there was enough of a common understanding of the requirements of the task that I was able to commence the actual research project.

The first formulation of the project, which I discussed with the research committee in March, took the form of a two-page description under the topic "A Study Encompassing the Geographical, Language and Cultural Identity of Minor Ethnic Groups in East New Britain". It enumerated three objectives:

- To identify and establish the geographical, language and cultural activities as means of identity for the various ethnic groups in the Pomio/Baining areas;
- To assess the effectiveness of these languages and cultural activities in promoting and sustaining the identities of the various ethnic groups;
- To identify and establish any reasons or factors responsible for the decline or improvements in the language and cultural activities as means of expression for ethnic group existence.

The document then went on to enumerate eight points in a draft terms of reference starting with the need to 'identify all clans/sub-clans by location, language, cultural activities etc.' and ending with 'to suggest possible policy initiatives for purposes of addressing the various needs of these ethnic groups in Provincial Government Planning'. This document, formulated by the research committee without my input, was discussed at several meetings. I recall these meetings as intense and focussed. My aim was as much as possible to get a sense of the significance of clan identity, for example, for the Tolai in particular and how these men, knowledgeable of conditions in other parts of the province, saw such concepts being played out in the lives of members of other ethnic groups. The end product of these meetings was a ten page document which, in a sense, deconstructed such notions as 'clan membership', 'traditional customs' and the like into concrete occurrences that had a bearing on the concerns of the committee. Over the next twelve months, I spent from over one month to five days in six villages in the Baining area and six villages in the Pomio area. These sites were selected by me in consultation with the research committee with the aim of gaining comparable material representing aspects of ethnic and cultural identity of all of the identified language groups of the province. My plan had been to spend one month at each site, so that I could at least approximate a traditional participant-observation methodology. This proved unrealistic in several instances because of expense, needs to conform to others' transport schedules, and sometimes political factors. In effect, I was doing cultural survey work and had to adjust my methodology to the exigencies of the particular situations.

Over that twelve-month period, I met with the research committee three times. At each meeting I distributed a discussion paper presenting my current findings and charting my progress in developing an analytical model. The final research report was submitted in July 1992 and I also addressed an assembly of senior government officials at which I circulated a summary of my findings with recommendations.

Methodological Considerations and the Development of Key Concepts

From my perspective, inherent in the project as described in the initial terms of reference were several conceptual problems. At base was a link between retention of traditional cultural activities as underlying identity and the notion of progress. I saw no necessary link between a strong cultural identity and economic progress except as illustrated in the case of the Tolai themselves. Very early on, it became clear that the standard of comparison and indeed, possibly a model held up to the other ethnic groups, were the Tolai. At this point I started to formulate and operationalize the concept of the 'successful ethnic group'. Thus, the government's desire to know about the retention of traditional cultural and linguistic differences, or lack thereof, plotted on a geographical plain and isomorphic with, it seemed to me, legitimate rights to some form of political autonomy, spoke to Tolai preoccupations. This one culture, one political unit model, which seemed to me inherent in government concerns may well reflect the ethno-nationalistic sentiments that were current in the region at the time. The secessionist movement in Bougainville had made a major impact on the political thinking of all the islands provinces. And ethno-nationalist movements had precipitated independence resulting in a provincial government system whose components were unevenly drawn around regionally dominant ethnic groups. Such identities were based on primordial values seen as immutable in contemporary multi-ethnic relations. I defined my task in developing the final terms of reference on the part of the research committee and me, as moving away from the essentialist, categorical understanding of ethnic identity associated with a primordial understanding of culture, to a more dynamic one where differences and similarities were negotiated in on the ground relationships (Barth 1994).

Largely, as a result of committee members speculating on the types of situations that I might encounter in my research or in recounting their own experiences, a much more self conscious understanding of contemporary cultural identity developed. For example, in the initial terms of reference one of the goals was phrased in terms of the decline or improvement of 'language and cultural activities as a means of expression for ethnic group existence'. In the final expanded version this item read:

Develop a description of characteristics which are believed by informants to typify their particular identity. These may be physical characteristics, personal qualities, types of ritual forms or specific practices in daily life. Use both male and female informants. Note generally held regional characterizations.

The allowance that cultural differences may be self-consciously and thus unevenly held, grew out of the shared recognition of the mutability of cultural identity itself in cases where Morobe plantation workers participated year after year in Baining festivals or an agricultural extension agent from the Sepik married into a Mengen village and negotiated old and new identities. Although this process brought our understandings of the phenomenon to be studied into greater agreement with the actual situation throughout the province at the time, the essentialist/relational dilemma still remained at the level of the idealized political organization of ethnic groups into free standing political entities. For example, another solution to the perceived problem of Baining identity was the institution of an exclusively Baining Community Government that would include all the Baining groups. However, I was able to put off my confrontation of the problem at this level until the completion of my research. At that point what could be seen as a theoretical issue in the conceptualization of ethnicity on the basis of cultural identity became a moral and ethical one with implications for the lives of real people.

Aside from the theoretical issues involved in discussions of culture and ethnicity (Borofsky 1994; Larmour 1992), the challenge to ethnographers to support the assertions of primordial cultural and ethnic identity on the part of peoples that we work with poses one of the major ethical dilemmas of our discipline. It is clear that the holding of an essentialist view of culture and ethnic identity has political consequences most readily apparent in applied contexts. This is particularly so in fourth world situations as van Meijl (2000) illustrates in his account of difficulties he encountered in working with a Maori community. Although he argues that what he calls a 'neo-modern conception of culture' has had a deep influence in academia, it is not easily accepted in instances where indigenous groups are asserting aboriginal claim (ibid. 100). In order to avoid such difficulties with the sponsors of my research, I pursued my task of moving my research project away from politically informed essentialisms through the consideration of my own research experiences. I was successful in doing this simply because the members of the research committee were open to the appreciation of a modernist identity at least as applicable to the minor ethnic groups of the province who were the subject of my research

I approached the problem from the perspective of the data-gathering event. I proposed that the significant difference in the understanding of ethnic identity and culture hinged on whether they were seen as a product of social relations or whether they were seen as based on attributes and/or a moral consciousness of a particular population. Further, drawing on my experience elsewhere in Papua New Guinea, I argued that ethnic identity would not be equally important in all social relations among all members of distinguishable groups (Comaroff 1987). I introduced this dichotomy into our discourse in the following manner. My first discussion paper opened with the following statement:

> The review of research completed on the survey of minor ethnic groups in the province to date has indicated the applicability of two distinct frameworks within which the data should be approached. These two frameworks hinge on distinct interpretations of the concept of ethnicity. On the one hand, there is the traditional anthropological understanding of ethnicity as based on essential cultural and linguistic differences which define and bound groups one from the other. (Rohatynskyj 1991:1)

The second concept of ethnicity I described as a dynamic one where interaction between communities mutually shaped particular identities and social realities. I argued that the value of attempting to understand individual cultures in their own terms lay in a type of salvage anthropology. The fact that many of the linguistic groups of the southwestern coast made no or little appearance in the ethnographic record was challenging and intriguing to both the research committee and to me. The value of the second approach lay in that it complemented the former by providing an understanding of group identity and practices within the reality of striving for economic development and pursuit of particular group interests. It thus allowed for inequality and the fact that one group may be dominant over the other, specifically by defining the common system within which all coexisted. Again, this thinking recognized the dominant position of the Tolai and secondarily the Mengen in the southwestern part of the province.

What I am struck by in this consideration of my efforts to elucidate to Tolai civil servants the difference between the essentialist and relational approaches, is the importance of this research experience in enabling me to realize that different kinds of situations called forth these two different approaches in my own work. In relation to my long-term concern with sex affiliation among the Ömie of the Northern (Oro) Province of Papua New Guinea, after a visit in 1990, I wrote an article which attempted to come to terms with my astonishment that I could no longer carry out the type of research I did among them on the eve of independence. I was particularly concerned that an internal system which seemed to have accounted for the uniqueness of the Ömie culture was no longer adequate to account for the dynamics of village life that I encountered in my revisit. I was concerned with the self-consciousness of cultural identity which seemed to me qualitatively different from the attitudes to traditional customs held by the community during my original research. Thus I wrote:

> There is no question that before Ömie recognized differences in language and custom between themselves and their neighbours. But the establishment of the Australian colonial administration facilitated the conceptualization of ethnic groups as a cluster comprising a system where differences in custom could be

evaluated in relation to the seemingly absolute economic and political power of the colonialist. (Rohatynskyj 1997:440)

The colonial administration thus created a framework, I argued, that contained a universe of ethnic groups and cultures which were comparable one with the other forming a stable multi-ethnic system as the administration buffered and absorbed all threats of dominance by any one of the units. This political buffering contributed to my ability to maintain a realist stance in ethnography in the 1970s in my first encounter with the Ömie.

The situation on the Gazelle Peninsula was quite different in the early 1990s. In addressing the 'Baining problem' in terms of the nature of the ethnography generated by the local context I have argued that Baining could not find a forum where they could objectify their cultural selves to their benefit. There was no equanimous display of relative difference possible in that particular setting.

> The situation on the Gazelle was historically unique: a product of complex political and economic forces. The Baining suffered for having one significant neighbor, and only one, in comparison with whom they became a negative absolute. By contrast, in the ethnographies of the Tolai mentioned earlier, the Tolai tended to compare favorably, not necessarily just with the Baining, but with Europeans as well. (Rohatynskyj 2000:190)

Thus, the research I conducted in the early 1990s, both academic and 'applied', allowed me to place the two understandings of ethnic identity and culture in relation to the sociopolitical situation encountered by the ethnographer. The essentialist understanding could be seen as called out in a particular period in the history of the Ömie dependent, at least in part, on the colonial government's superordinate function as equalizing and containing difference in comparable units. The shift to a relational perspective could be seen as necessitated by the removal of that framework and the freeing of dominating tendencies of some of the ethnic groups previously contained. Historicizing the opposition in the specific context of the Northern (Oro) Province allowed me to come to terms with the importance of historical context in shaping our research results. I have argued that the Tolai were never the subjects of a traditional, self-contained village ethnography simply because issues of integration into larger superordinate structures were called out much earlier in relation to them than in the mountainous part of the Northern (Oro) Province or, for that matter, on the periphery of the road network of the Gazelle where the Baining resided (Rohatynskyj 2000). It is perhaps this tendency on the part of the Tolai, unlike the Baining and the Ömie, to enter modern ethnography as coeval with the researcher, living in the same world and the same time, that contributed to their positive evaluation in the regional system and in ethnographic discourse.

The structure of the mutually arrived at conceptual framework for my research into the causes of the lack of development of the minor ethnic groups of the Province of East New Britain, recognized both Tolai economic and political dominance and the hegemonic position that they had acquired in the formulation of research questions in the area. This was done by formally operationalizing the concept of a 'successful ethnic group' as the standard for my research of the minor ethnic groups. The introductory pages of my report consider the process of developing the final terms of reference and arrive at the following definition of parameters of 'success' as the basis for comparison.

> Inherent in the phrasing of the goals of the project and the terms of reference then was an implication of a model of a 'successful' ethnic group in relation to which some of the minor ethnic groups of the province were found wanting. Some of the characteristics of a successful ethnic group can be discerned from even a cursory examination of the terms within which the research project has been phrased. A successful ethnic group within the context of present day Papua New Guinean life would be one that had a clear and highly valued sense of identity, a retention of certain selected aspects of traditional culture, including the vernacular language, which were displayed with pride as symbols of that ethnic identity, and lastly, the ability to adapt and turn to their own advantage the vast economic and political changes that had taken place in the lives of its members. Without having to cast about too far, it is clear that the Tolai present themselves as an example of such an ethnic group both in their own evaluation and in that of others. (Rohatynskyj 1992:5)

Modernist Identity and Ethnography

As I was writing my report in mid-1992, I was struggling with issues that other anthropologists had confronted and conceptualized in a much more elegant manner than I. In the years since the completion of my work for the province, I have come to appreciate the degree to which the very representation of ethnographic research entails theoretical and conceptual issues. George Marcus (1992:312) succinctly identifies the dichotomy that I was attempting to explicate to the sponsors of my research as emerging 'from a systematic *disqualification* of the various structuring devices on which ethnographic realism has depended'. The ongoing deconstruction of the solidity of the basis of difference, such as kinship affiliation, traditional territory *etc.*, through the operation of global forces, he sees as problematizing the spatial, temporal and perspectival tropes of realist ethnography. In relation to the spatial dimension, he comments:

> Cultural difference or diversity arises here not from some local struggle for identity, but as a function of a complex process among all the sites in which the identity of someone or a group anywhere is defined in simultaneity. It is the

burden of the modernist ethnography to capture distinctive identity forma-
tions in all their migrations and dispersion. This multi-locale, dispersed identity vision thus reconfigures and complexifies the spatial plane on which
ethnography has conceptually operated. (Marcus 1992:316)

In my struggle to fulfill the terms of reference to the satisfaction of the
sponsors, I was forced to confront the limitations of a realist ethnography
based on primordial identities, in favor of a multi-locale perspective
amenable to a modernist treatment. This was required by the very structure of my research strategy, survey work. Although I had conducted survey work before, gathering bits of information from a number of locations
and samples of populations in West Africa as a consultant for various gender and development projects, the subject matter of the current research
did not allow for a discrete treatment of localized findings. Indeed, the
information that was of most interest to me was that which implicated
identity at other sites thus cross-cutting and negating geography itself.

The subject matter of my concern and the time and resource limitations under which I was working, shaped what I see as the final product
of my research. This was a sketch of a system of ethnic relations within
the confines of the provincial territory but based on a comprehension of
the large scale exogenous and historical forces, both economic and political, that determined a hierarchy of ethnic groups in the province. My
second discussion paper presented to the research committee proposed a
hierarchy of successful ethnic groups of which the foremost was the Tolai
having dominance over the entire province from the metropolitan center
of Rabaul-Kokopo dependent on its immediate hinterland populated by
the Baining. I identified a secondary metropolitan center associated with
the Mengen ethnic group at Pomio-Mal Mal which enjoyed its own sphere
of dominance in the Mengen populations of the inland center of the
province. The dominance of the Mengen ethnic group was expressed in
the pervasiveness of the Pomio Kivung (Whitehouse 1995) among the
inland populations and the Kivung itself posed a political challenge to
the Tolai both within the province and on the national scene.[4] The third,
relatively successful ethnic group, I identified, was that of the Lote, which
was based at Uvol close to the southwestern border of the province.
Again, it dominated its own hinterland and seemed to me to be caught in
a careful negotiation of fealty between the Catholic Church and the
Pomio Kivung. This world systems approach confined to the province
can be seen as a result of the kind of multi-sited ethnography designed to
capture the simultaneity of identity construction in a deterritorialized
world but where territory itself is highly contested as a source of both
power and identity (Marcus 1994).

My concern in carrying out this type of research and the reason I had
hoped to spend at least one month in each of the research sites, was that
I would not have sufficient time to capture a perspective from any one

particular location. Traditional ethnographic research, based on long-term participant observation, necessitates a type of local knowledge that is only gained through time and experience (Hastrup 1995). In short, I was afraid that my research would be superficial. And indeed, it was in terms of any particular group. For I can not make any in depth, authoritative statement about the nature of the culture of the Kol, for example, or of the Maenge, or of the Chachet Baining. Although, I can make relatively informed statements about the attitude of these ethnic groups to symbols of their traditional culture and the group's relative positioning within the hierarchy of the provincial ethnic system. At issue are two different kinds of ethnographic knowledge gained from two different positions; the one provided depth and detail, the other a grasp of the scope of activities that impinge on the local and immediate.

The consequence of my methodology was an appreciation of the structuring of ethnography in terms of regional identity politics. Of special interest here are the Baining who have historically been held in low esteem by just about everyone and provided a daunting challenge to a number of ethnographers, among them Gregory Bateson, in terms of discerning a unique culture.[5] The conclusion of all my grappling with the 'Baining problem' initiated by my work for the Department of East New Britain, is an appreciation of the particular configuration of the ethnic system of the Gazelle as shaping Baining identity. Referring to my work on the question of minor ethnic groups in East New Britain, I later wrote:

> The examination of the historical conditions that generated the present subordination of the Baining in the politics and economy of the Gazelle Peninsula demonstrates that the ethnographic representation of the Baining by Bateson was shaped by these very conditions to the same degree that my interaction with them was shaped by Baining challenge to these conditions. In as much as we speak of techniques, methods, and fieldwork know-how, our subject matter escapes us and becomes entangled in the very history that frames our encounters. Bateson's "failure" with the Baining is not a personal failure but rather an instance of the inability of the researcher to transcend the power of the historical forces shaping the cultural identity of the native in the regional system. (Rohatynskyj 2000:191–192)

If the Tolai served as a model of the 'successful ethnic group' that structured my research for the provincial government, then clearly the Baining were an example of a 'failed ethnic group'. The codification of such a dramatic contrast was brought out by their proximity and the appreciation of the historical and economic forces which generated such an underdeveloped hinterland to the prosperous metropolitan center of the province.

Ethics and Racialism

The Tolai government's acceptance of the suggestion that there was an element of racialism at the heart of Tolai/Baining relations and that it impacted the current understanding of the 'Baining problem' was due to their acceptance, based on their own experiences of ethnic identity in the province, of the tenets of a modernist identity in Marcus's terms. This acceptance may well be related to the length of their history as self-perceived and generally recognized coeval actors in a modernist world. My definition of racialism for purposes of the report was quite simplistic having to do with differences of kind as opposed to degree. Racialism is as much a contested concept as are ethnicity and culture. Jonathan Friedman (1994:30) in talking about the properties of global systems sees both race and Western (modern) ethnicity as ascribed, carried in or on the body, as it were, as opposed to Traditional ethnicity and Lifestyle, which are achieved through individual activity. Karen Brodkin (2000:241) in trying to understand the ascription of 'not-quite-white' status to various ethnic groups in the United States historically sees race, as well as ethnicity, class and gender as mutually constituting political and economic relationships of capitalism. I do not propose to untangle these threads here, although I see this as a future project.

However, the evocation of this highly charged term in my final report to the research committee and the senior members of the government, was a strategy as much as a scientific finding. The opposition between a primordial identity tied to the land and a relational one, mutually engaging and allowing for inequality, was bridged by a research strategy that could encompass them both. However, the same opposition between a primordial identity and a relational one at the level of policy recommendations called forth an ethical conscience on my part. The two solutions that were touted at the time to rising Baining militancy growing out of the 'Baining problem' were an Office of Minor Ethnic Groups or an all Baining Community Government. I saw serious problems with both of these proposals. Both of them necessitated the recognition of a special status for the Baining based on a perception of disadvantage in relation to other ethnic groups. Although it is possible to argue that such policy initiatives allow for remedial services for the targeted group, they could potentially also further disadvantage them by robbing them of the generally held rights of other citizens. It was my stance that whatever difference was perceived by government officials between themselves and the Baining had to be addressed in terms of degree of difference. In a sense I wanted to keep definitions of difference in relative terms of economic disadvantage, relative lack of access to education, relative isolation from the road network of the Gazelle. I felt that the codification of perceived differences in terms of kind would further strengthen the perception of the 'Baining problem' as having nothing to do with the Tolai themselves, reinforcing racialist beliefs and perceptions of Baining identity as immutable and somehow in or on the body. I was concerned to maintain the policy recognition of differences between Tolai and Baining as commensurate as opposed to incommensurate to borrow Gewertz and Errington's (1999) terms used in discussing the hardening of class distinctions in contemporary Papua New Guinea. Thus in my final summary and presentation to senior government officials I discouraged the incorporation into the constitution of the province the issue of ethnicity and cultural identity and argued for the value of approaching the 'Baining problem' through the concept of 'citizens of the province'. My findings and recommendations were accepted with respect. I do not know that any action was taken on my specific recommendations prior to the catastrophic events of September 1994 and the restructuring of the provincial system itself.

Reflections on the Consultancy Experience

In rereading this reflexive consideration of the consultancy experience it is very clear that the problems that were presented to me by the contractor engaged a number of threads that had been developing in my 'academic' research. I have quoted from academic publications written both before and after the various reports I wrote for the research committee of the Department of East New Britain. It is clear to me, but perhaps only suggested by the direct quotations selected, that there is a continuity in these works and that both types of writings are preoccupied with the same problems. Indeed, the one research setting feeds into the other.

I have distinguished this consultancy experience from academic research by drawing on the model of the generation of ethnographic texts developed by Sjoerd Jaarsma and me (Rohatynskyj and Jaarsma 2000). Whereas every ethnographic artifact is generated in the vortex of relationships between the researcher, the community under study and the audience for which the ethnography is written, in cases of contracted research the relationship between the audience and the researcher takes precedence in shaping the final outcome. However, I have contended that this does not obviate the ethical responsibility that the researcher has to the 'native', the community under study. In the case of the present research, I have argued that by developing the concept of a 'successful ethnic group' as a standard for the examination of the conditions of the 'minor ethnic groups' of the province, I brought the conditions of research and the subject of research into the same discourse. This allowed me to present an analysis of the plight of the more disadvantaged groups of the province which implicated the dominant Tolai. Recent discussions of ethics in the discipline have emphasized the responsibility to the sponsors of the research (Fluehr-Lobban 1991). This is no doubt a function of the number of anthropologists who are working as consultants in the present.

However, this stance does not subsume previous concerns about the responsibility to the host community as highlighted by Redcliffe (1985).

The point is that obligations to the one need not be cancelled by obligations to the other. The ethics of academic research are not so clearly distinguishable from those of contracted research, especially as we have come to appreciate the long- and short-term impact of our ethnographic writings on the identity construction of groups within regional and global systems. This is particularly the case in the body of work that I have been discussing, concerned with ethnic identity *per se*. Our ability to fulfill our ethical obligations to both the populations of our study and to possible sponsors of research as well as other types of audience, hinges on our appreciation of the nature of modernist identity and modernist ethnography. Contemporary ethnography in Oceania, whether contracted or not, embroils the researcher in intricate overlaps of self and other, partial identifications and complex distributions of sympathy. It demands of individual researchers the ability to both challenge and respect the essentialisms constructed as part of the strategies of others to assert claims and redress wrongs.

Acknowledgments

I was a research officer in the Division of Planning and Technical Services of the Department of East New Britain from February 1991 to July 1992. I was given permission to publish my research as long as I acknowledged the Department of East New Britain. I thank the then Premier of the Province, the Honorable Sinai Brown O.B.E., and the then first secretary, Mr. Ellison Kaivovo O.B.E., for their support of my research. I thank all the communities in the Pomio/Baining areas for their cooperation and participation. I would like to also thank the two anonymous readers for the journal for their very valuable comments and suggestions, and Pamela Stewart and Andrew Strathern for helping to bring this essay to publication.

Notes

1. Realist ethnography according to Marcus and others that use the term is defined by the acceptance of community and identity as based on shared values and shared culture mapped on a single locality. There is an acceptance of both homogeneity and solidity in this understanding of identity and community, and a boundedness of the process of identity formation within the terms of the community itself. One of the outcomes of a realist ethnography is a profound understanding of the behavior and customs of the people of a particular locality and an explanation of their interactions in the world with others as based on an identity very much created and dictated by that place alone.
2. My discussion of the political and economic realities of the Gazelle is restricted to the period immediately before the volcanic eruptions which commenced in September

1994. That event and the restructuring of the provincial government system in the nation as a whole, have had a profound impact on these conditions.

3. I do not know if the government would have contracted an independent consultant to investigate the issues of ethnicity and underdevelopment if the position had not been supported by the Canadian non-governmental organization, CUSO.

4. Whitehouse (1995) describes Kivung and Kivung-related activity among Mali, one of the southern groups of the Baining. This seems to be the only Baining community that was influenced by the cult. On the other hand, most speakers of languages of the Mengen Language Family, further to the south are at the present or have been in the recent past, members of the Kivung.

5. Jane Fajans (1997) has provided a creative solution to the inability of ethnographers to apprehend a unique Baining culture by a theoretical approach that recognizes the 'emergent' nature of cultural forms from mundane and play activities.

References

Barth, F. 1994 "A Personal View of Present Tasks and Priorities in Cultural and Social Anthropology". In R. Borofsky (ed) *Assessing Cultural Anthropology*. New York: McGraw-Hill.

Borofsky, R. (ed) 1994 *Assessing Cultural Anthropology*. New York: McGraw-Hill.

Brodkin, K. 2000 "Global Capitalism: What's Race Got to Do With It?" 1998 AES Keynote Address, *American Ethnologist* 27(2): 237–256.

Comaroff, J.L. 1987 "Of Totemism and Ethnicity: Consciousness, Practice and the Signs of Inequality". *Ethnos* 52: 301–323.

East New Britain Provincial Government 1977 Constitution of the East New Britain Province, Rabaul, East New Britain, Papua New Guinea.

Epstein, A.L. 1969 *Matupit: Land, Politics and Change among the Tolai of New Britain*. Canberra: Australian National University Press.

———— 1979 "Tambu: The Shell-Money of the Tolai". In R.H. Hook (ed) *Fantasy and Symbol: Studies in Anthropological Interpretation*. Essays in honour of Georges Devereux. London: Academic Press.

————1999 *Gunantuna: Aspects of the Person, the Self and the Individual among the Tolai*. Bathurst, Australia: Crawford House Publishing.

Epstein, T.S. 1968 *Capitalism: Primitive and Modern: Some Aspects of Tolai Economic Growth*. East Lansing: Michigan State University Press.

Errington, F. K. and D. B. Gewertz 1995 *Articulating Change in the "Last Unknown"*. Boulder, San Francisco, Oxford: Westview Press.

Fabian, J. 1994 "Ethnographic Objectivity Revisited: From Rigor to Vigor". In A. Megill (ed) *Rethinking Objectivity*. Durham, N.C.: Duke University Press.

Fajans, J. 1997 *They Make Themselves: Work and Play among the Baining of Papua New Guinea*. Chicago and London: The University of Chicago Press.

Fluehr-Lobban, C. 1991 "Ethics and Professionalism: A Review of Issues and Principles within Anthropology". In C. Fleuhr-Lobban (ed) *Ethics and the Profession of Anthropology: Dialogue for a New Era*. Philadelphia: University of Pennsylvania Press.

Friedman, J. 1994 *Cultural Identity and Global Process*. London, Thousand Oaks, New Delhi: Sage Publications.

Gewertz, D.B. and F.K. Errington 1999 *Emerging Class in Papua New Guinea: The Telling of Difference*. Cambridge: Cambridge University Press.

Grosart, I. 1982 "Nationalism and Micronationalism: The Tolai Case". In R. May (ed) *Micronationalist Movements in Papua New Guinea*. Canberra: Australian National University.

Hastrup, K. 1995 *A Passage to Anthropology: Between Experience and Theory*. London: Routledge.

Hempenstall, P.J. 1978 *Pacific Islanders under German Rule: A Study in the Meaning of Colonial Resistance.* Canberra: Australian National University Press.

Larmour, P. 1992 "The Politics of Race and Ethnicity: Theoretical Perspectives on Papua New Guinea". *Pacific Studies* 15(2):87–108.

Marcus, G. 1992 "Past, Present and Emergent Identities: Requirements for Ethnographies of Late Twentieth-Century Modernity Worldwide". In S. Lash and J. Friedman (eds) *Modernity and Identity.* Oxford: Blackwell.

——— 1994 "The Modernist Sensibility in Recent Ethnographic Writing and the Cinematic Metaphor of Montage". In L. Taylor (ed) *Visualizing Theory: Selected Essays from V.A.R. 1990–1994.* London: Routledge.

Neumann, K. 1992 *Not the Way It Really Was: Constructing the Tolai Past.* Honolulu: University of Hawaii Press.

——— 1996 *Rabaul: Yu Swit Moa Yet.* Oxford: Oxford University Press.

Post-Courier 1991 *Bids to Preserve Tolai Culture.* Port Moresby, November 4:16.

Redcliffe, M.R. 1985 "Policy Research and Anthropological Compromise: Should the Piper Call the Tune?" In R. Grillo and A. Rew (eds) *Social Anthropology and Development Policy.* London and New York: Tavistock Publications.

Rohatynskyj, M. 1991 "Minor Ethnic Groups: Discussion Paper Number One". December 10, 1991, Division of Planning and Technical Services, Department of East New Britain, Rabaul, East New Britain, Papua New Guinea.

——— 1992 *A Study of Minor Ethnic Groups in East New Britain.* July 1992, Report to the Department of East New Britain, Rabaul, East New Britain, Papua New Guinea.

——— 1997 "Culture, Secrets, and Ömie History: A Consideration of the Politics of Cultural Identity". *American Ethnologist* 24(2): 438–456.

Rohatynskyj, M.A. 2000 "The Enigmatic Baining: The Breaking of an Ethnographer's Heart". In S.R. Jaarsma and M.A. Rohatynskyj (eds) *Ethnographic Artifacts: Challenges to a Reflexive Anthropology.* Honolulu: University of Hawaii Press.

Rohatynskyj, M.A. and S.R. Jaarsma 2000 "Introduction: Ethnographic Artifacts". In S.R. Jaarsma and M.A. Rohatynskyj (eds) *Ethnographic Artifacts: Challenges to a Reflexive Anthropology.* Honolulu: University of Hawaii Press.

Salisbury, R.F. 1970 *Vunamami: Economic Transformation in a Traditional Society.* Berkeley: University of California Press.

Van Meijl, T. 2000 "The Politics of Ethnography in New Zealand". In S.R. Jaarsma and M.A. Rohatynskyj (eds) *Ethnographic Artifacts: Challenges to a Reflexive Anthropology.* Honolulu: University of Hawaii Press.

Whitehouse, H. 1995 *Inside the Cult: Religious Innovation and Transmission in Papua New Guinea.* Oxford: Oxford University Press.

Chapter 2

FROM ANTHROPOLOGIST TO GOVERNMENT OFFICER AND BACK AGAIN

Richard Scaglion

In June 1979, I prepared excitedly to return to Papua New Guinea. I had been hired by the Public Services Commission to direct a Customary Law Development Project for the Law Reform Commission. I had previously conducted anthropological field research in the country, examining customary law and legal change among the Abelam people in what, when I began my work, was the East Sepik District of Australia's Territory of Papua and New Guinea. I remained there from 1974–1976, experiencing the end of the colonial period, which terminated formally on September 16, 1975. I had begun my research in the country as an anthropologist. Now I was to return as a government officer.

Papua New Guinea had adopted the Australian legal system in force on Independence day in 1975 as an interim national legal system. However, Western law often clashed with the customary law of tribal peoples within the newly independent country. For this reason, national leaders sought to develop a self-reliant national legal system that would be based on Melanesian customs and traditions rather than on those of their former colonial administrators. It was obvious from the outset that this would be a prolonged and difficult task, because Papua New Guinea is well known for its cultural diversity. According to Grimes (1992), there are at least 862 mutually unintelligible languages spoken in the country, and at least as many customary legal systems. Amid such diversity, would it be possible to uncover underlying legal principles shared by many of these Melanesian societies? Could the essence of Melanesian customary law, which developed in small-scale tribal societies, be reconciled with the requirements of a modern nation-state?

References for this chapter begin on page 61.

In order to address these and other questions on a long-term basis, a Law Reform Commission was established as a constitutional body with responsibility to "investigate and report to the Parliament and to the National Executive on the development, and on the adaptation to the circumstances of the country, of the underlying law, and on the appropriateness of the rules and principles of the underlying law to the circumstances of the country". Recognizing that an understanding of customary law was critical to developing an underlying law appropriate for Papua New Guinea, the Law Reform Commission designed a basic framework for a Customary Law Development Project to investigate the nature of customary law and the extent to which it could be used as the basis for a unique national legal system.

In 1978, I was a relatively newly hired Assistant Professor of Anthropology at the University of Pittsburgh. Knowing of my interest in legal development in Papua New Guinea (Scaglion 1976), officers of the Law Reform Commission selected me to direct the Customary Law Project. I was expected to design an ongoing research strategy to gather data on customary law, analyze the data, identify problem areas, and help create draft legislation designed to help alleviate difficulties. I was also expected to help train nationals to carry on the research after I left. In short, I was offered the opportunity to help design and initiate a broad policy direction for nationwide legal development. I found this prospect very appealing, and was extremely enthusiastic about the post.

Unfortunately, academic schedules rarely mesh smoothly with the needs of consulting clients, and this opportunity was no exception. A complicated timetable had to be worked out before I could accept the position. The Public Services Commission had initially authorized a three-year posting. However, because secondment is not widely practiced in the United States, my permanent academic position there did not allow me to take a continuous three-year leave of absence. After considerable discussion between officers of the Law Reform Commission and the Department of Justice on the one hand, and myself, my wife and children, my department and university, and my wife's school district (she was an elementary school teacher), we finally reached an agreement that divided the project into phases. I would take up the post by June 1979 and would work through August 1980, a period of fifteen months, during which time I would get the project underway and supervise data gathering. I would then take official leave from my government post for nine months and teach a full academic year at the University of Pittsburgh while at the same time analyzing the data gathered during the first phase of the project. The data-analysis facilities at the University of Pittsburgh were superior to anything present in Papua New Guinea at the time, so this would actually save time and money for the government. I would then return to my government post in April 1981, remain for nine months to write up preliminary results, return to Pittsburgh to teach for one term, and then return to Papua New Guinea as a consultant for another four months to begin work on draft legislation. Afterwards, if the Law Reform Commission and I both thought it would be profitable, I agreed to return again as a consultant to finish up any remaining work the next North American summer, after teaching another full academic year.

This may sound quite complicated, but it seemed workable enough to me and to the officers of the Law Reform Commission and the University of Pittsburgh. I pointed out that between 1979–1982 I would be spending more than two years total time in the country. Because my job as Assistant Professor of Anthropology had a research component, I could be doing considerable work for the Law Reform Commission while I was in the United States; work which, I hastened to point out, would be free to the government of Papua New Guinea. So the Law Reform Commission would be getting some three years of my effort, spread out over a total period of four years, and paying for somewhat less than two and one-half years of my time. The University, for their part, agreed to give me three terms unpaid leave of absence, so that I could take advantage of this opportunity. It seemed like a good arrangement all around. I was issued with an initial two-year contract, which we understood would be fulfilled in fifteen-month and nine-month installments, and I prepared to take up my post.

Logistical Difficulties in Port Moresby

In newly independent Papua New Guinea, most contract officers, especially in the Justice Department, were long-term Australian public servants who had moved with their families and belongings to spend a minimum of three years in the country. Most had lived there for much longer, and had had most of their worldly possessions shipped to them. On the other hand, I arrived in Port Moresby, the capital city of Papua New Guinea, with a single suitcase in May 1979. I was to set up a household alone, since my wife and children would arrive in July, after the end of the school year. Upon arrival I discovered that, contrary to assurances made to me by officers of the Law Reform Commission, no house had yet been allocated for me and my family. I bought a car, stayed in a conveniently located hotel (paid for from my project budget), and began my work. Without belaboring the details, the allocation and renovation of a suitable government house required herculean efforts on my part to accomplish, and when my wife and children arrived, I still did not have my house. We were to continue living in a hotel for another full month (the costs still charged against my project budget) before finally moving into our new home. Requisitioning and arranging for delivery of the major furniture and appliances provided by the government was another serious problem, and it was a full five months after arriving in Papua New Guinea before I had a fully functioning home and could really settle into my work.

I also had some problems with various government regulations. I quickly came to realize that, unlike the Patrol Officers whom I had met and befriended on my first trip to the Territory of Papua and New Guinea, most Australian expatriate contract officers in Port Moresby held desk jobs, and Public Service guidelines were very strict about monitoring absences from the office. For legal researchers, this was rarely a problem, since the Justice Department enjoyed a very complete law library. But it was a real problem for my research. First of all, the archival and library resources that I needed for my work were located elsewhere in the city. The Law Reform Commission was housed in the Development Bank Building, apart from other government offices, whereas most anthropological materials needed for my work were located at the University of Papua New Guinea, which was near my house. This would seem to be a convenient arrangement, but it was not. Regulations required me to drive to the Development Bank Building, check in at the office at 6:45 a.m., then sign out and return to where I had come from to begin my actual work. If I spent the entire day at the University, I still had to make the long round trip at rush hour to return to the office merely to check out at 4:06 p.m. I really began to appreciate the freedom of the academic setting I had left behind.

The archival research that I was able to complete despite these obstacles revealed a bias in the literature on customary law in New Guinea. Most of the materials that I located either were old, or had been gathered by anthropologists working in relatively unacculturated parts of the country. What was missing were contemporary studies of customary law in areas where the process of reconciling national law and customary law was well underway. It became obvious that we would have to arrange to have such data gathered specifically for the project. I investigated several alternative strategies, including making use of magistrates, foreign anthropologists, and/or lawyers, and finally decided on hiring students from the University of Papua New Guinea to work in their home areas during their long year-end break. These students already spoke the local language and were familiar with the cultural setting. I also believed that their descriptions of their own customary legal systems were more likely to reflect indigenous categories than if, say, Australian lawyers had done the research.

I selected a group of twenty University students, designed an instructional format and minicourse, and began training students in anthropological data-gathering techniques. I stressed the importance of collecting extended conflict cases (see e.g. Nader and Todd 1978:5–8) for the elicitation of primary data. Although it was sensible to train the students at the University, where they were living and studying, I again had to be absent from my office in the Development Bank Building on an almost daily basis, with all of the attendant bureaucratic problems. After completing the training phase, the students scattered to their home areas to begin their investigations. During this actual research phase, I attempted to supervise the student researchers in the field. This time I was absent from the office for weeks at a time, traveling throughout the country. This required reams of paperwork and produced considerable logistical problems. Travel was very difficult and time-consuming, especially in rural areas with no reliable infrastructure.

Conceptual Difficulties in Port Moresby

I also realized soon after I began my project that the legal officers in the Justice Department had a very different conception of customary law and how it operates from what was standard anthropological orthodoxy. I believe many of them imagined that my project would provide them with discrete compendiums or restatements of principles of law in various societies, such as had been attempted in colonial Africa. But apart from the impossibility of preparing 862 different restatements, the practice of conflict management as it actually unfolds in the comparatively egalitarian societies of Papua New Guinea is very flexible—which is really its strength. Most local groups rarely refer to abstract rules or precedents when settling conflict cases. Instead, decisions are reached on a case-by-case basis through bargaining and consensus. Cases that look similar from the vantage point of Western law may be handled quite differently depending on such factors as the social relationships between parties to the dispute, the relative status of the main actors in the case, and the unique conflict history of the dispute. The idea of the "blind scales of justice" of Western society, in which all individuals are equal under the law, makes no sense to people for whom the relationship between parties to a dispute is of paramount importance. Customary law in New Guinea is less a system of application of formal rules to a given fact situation and more a system for insuring a just solution through compromise. Furthermore, the very flexibility of customary law allows it to be responsive to changing social conditions. Formal and detailed restatements of customary law, once they were given the force of law, would freeze customary law at a single and quickly outdated point in time and destroy flexibility. Yet in Papua New Guinea, where social change was and continues to be very rapid, an adaptable legal system is of paramount importance.

Legal anthropologists often distinguish between *substantive law* (rules for normative behavior, infractions of which are negatively sanctioned) and *procedural law* (mechanisms through which legal issues are actually handled). Pospisil (e.g. 1971:2) has frequently pointed out that the English term "law" really consists of two separate concepts that are distinguished in many other languages. For example in Latin, *lex* is an abstract rule usually made explicit in a legal code, whereas *ius* refers to the underlying principles implied in actual case decisions. Whereas lawyers are often preoccupied with *leges* (plural of *lex*; the statutory rules), anthropologists (and Melanesians) tend to be more interested in the procedures by which disputes actually get settled, and with the underlying principles of fairness implied in such settlements.

The consequences of taking these different approaches to "law" became apparent in a practical arena that directly affected my work: the assessment of Papua New Guinea's newly established Village Courts. Village Courts, meant to be a forum in which customary and introduced law could be blended together, were established in Papua New Guinea by the *Village Courts Act* 1973 (No. 12 of 1974). As described in section 18, the primary function of a Village Court is "to ensure peace and harmony in the area for which it is established by mediating in and endeavoring to obtain just and amicable settlements of disputes" by applying relevant native custom. Previous to the establishment of Village Courts, the lowest officially recognized judicial body in the Territory was the Local Court, which was based on Western principles and employed Western law. But earlier anthropological research (e.g. Scaglion 1976 and M. Strathern 1972) showed that local people often avoided having their grievances aired in this forum because they were uncomfortable with introduced law and legal procedures. They preferred to have their disputes aired in villages using customary practices. A mimeographed report entitled "The History of Village Courts in Papua New Guinea", prepared by the Village Courts Secretariat, makes it clear that among the reasons for establishing these courts was the rejection of Local Courts by village people. In contrast, the Village Courts were intended to employ the customary dispute resolution practices that were actually used in the villages, but to have dispute case solutions accorded the weight of law by empowering traditional leaders to act as Local Court Magistrates.

When I began my work with the Law Reform Commission, Village Courts were just being established in many parts of the country. Despite the seemingly obvious advantages of a system of justice that enabled people to litigate according to custom but still be operating within the boundaries of a national legal system, Village Courts were a hard sell to many of the lawyers in Papua New Guinea at the time. Some felt that different customary principles being applied in different locations would only lead to confusion and decentralization, and that there should be a single rule of written law for everyone everywhere. Others thought that Village Courts were too "formal", that Village Court Magistrates exercised more adjudication than mediation in their decision-making, that they mimicked Local Courts in their procedures, and that they strengthened the position of local elites. Still others took what Galanter (1981:1) has called a "legal centralism" perspective, in which law is seen as an instrument of domination of an essentially powerless peasantry by a ruling class (see, e.g. Fitzpatrick 1980). Thus, Paliwala (1982:191), in an analysis of Papua New Guinea's Village Courts, thought that they brought about "greater involvement and control by the state and a degree of authoritarianism on the part of court officials. The result is relatively alienated dispute settlement with little scope for community involvement and party consensus". Paliwala and Weisbrot (1982:12) went one step further in contending that, "In the end, the kind of society that [Papua New Guinea] is becoming will have more to do with the political economy of dependence than with the reform of the legal system".

As an anthropologist, I felt that the Village Courts could provide an excellent forum in which customary and introduced law could be blended together. Shortly after taking up my post as Director of Customary Law for the Law Reform Commission, I had returned to my field site in the Sepik foothills to do pilot research on legal changes in the area that had occurred since my 1974–1976 work, and to design a practical methodology for the student researchers to follow. I observed the newly established Village Courts in the area, and was very impressed with how well they seemed to be working (Scaglion 1979). This was in stark contrast to what the lawyers were saying, so I consulted with other anthropologists who had had long-term research experience in the country. Their research seemed to corroborate what I had found.

Anthropologists interested in law have often taken what I have called an "interactive model of legal pluralism" (Scaglion 1990:18). They see local people not so much as an oppressed peasantry, but rather as legal innovators who are quite able to affect their own affairs. In fact, Melanesian customary law has always been flexible enough to incorporate social change. But because the Village Courts had just begun operations, not much had yet been published from an anthropological perspective. However, anthropologists whom I knew reported verbally on seeing more complex interactions between customary and introduced law in Village Courts in their field sites that the legal centralists believed. Fortunately, I was able to consult with them, and to profit from their advice. A. J. Strathern, for example, had conducted field research in 1977 and had observed Village Courts. In a book published later (1984:64), but based on this work, Strathern stated:

> A point which must be stressed here, as earlier, is that *all* activities in the Highlands nowadays are of a "mixed" character. When we say that Village Courts reflect the capitalist economic system, this does not exclude the fact that they are also influenced by customary ideas and that the actual decisions they make reflect cultural conceptions about the person, shame, responsibility, and so on. Emphatically, they do reflect these ideas, but it is still significant that these courts have ordered fines to be paid as well as, or instead of, compensation to injured or aggrieved parties, as already mentioned. This indicates that the magistrates quite self-consciously realize they are operating an introduced, state-based institution and not just deciding disputes by "customary law".

George Westermark, whose Ph.D. research focused on legal pluralism and Village Courts in Agarabi (1978, 1981), had also seen evidence that Village Courts were effectively blending together customary and introduced law.

He had seen that the Village Courts were part of a wider arena of conflict management options, that litigants had choices in pursuing their options, and that they often chose Village Courts. He saw how Village Court Magistrates creatively used mediation techniques to settle disputes as envisioned in the original Village Courts Act. Anthropologists Robert Gordon and Mervyn Meggitt (1985:221), also reporting on earlier research, cited the testimony of an Engan man: "The Village Courts here are doing an excellent job. Most of the decisions are a compromise with the new government laws and the traditional laws. Other courts give less consideration to the customs and practices of the people, so today more court cases are heard by the Village Courts than by the Local Court in Laiagam". Indeed, based in part on this flexibility, Gordon and Meggitt concluded that "village courts have greater potential for dealing with the law-and-order problem [in Enga Province] than any of the other options considered" (1985:15–16).

Clearly, I was facing some very real problems in my work with the Justice Department. Apart from the logistical and bureaucratic difficulties that seemed to plague my use of anthropological research practices and techniques in a milieu seemingly designed for legal research in a law library, there were some very fundamental disagreements about the overall direction of my project. First, I wanted to focus on procedural law—the processes by which disputes were actually resolved, rather than on substantive law—the "rules" that most Melanesians seemed to lack but that the lawyers seemed to think were so important. Many of the other government legal officers did not feel that this was a profitable direction for me to take. In part because of my focus on dispute-management processes, I believed that Village Courts held much promise for reconciling customary and introduced law at the local level. I began to work closely with the Village Court Secretariat in order to help this process along. I consulted in the establishment and extension of the Village Courts system throughout the country, for example. Again, many of the lawyers in the Justice Department disagreed with this approach.

In the Village

As I mentioned earlier, in July 1979, shortly after taking up my government post, I returned to my field site in Neligum, an Abelam village in the Sepik foothills. I planned to conduct research on legal change, and to test various research methodologies for the student researchers to employ in their home areas. My return was a very happy homecoming for me. I had left Neligum three years earlier, after fifteen months of fieldwork that I remembered very fondly. The people of Neligum had welcomed me graciously, and had hosted me with a kindness that I can never repay. I eagerly anticipated reacquainting myself with my old friends there.

My initial fieldwork had been funded by a grant from the Center for Studies of Crime and Delinquency of the US Department of Health, Education and Welfare. While the funds they provided were adequate to support my most basic research expenses, I found myself operating on a very tight budget, as field anthropologists often do. Partially by inclination but mostly by necessity, I lived a life much like my hosts in Neligum. I lived in a house constructed of bush materials like everyone else. I ate whatever everyone else ate whenever they ate. When I traveled with my Abelam friends, we walked. When we wanted to go to Wewak, the District headquarters, we walked to the road and tried to hitch a ride with any passing vehicle, since there was no public transportation. Often we waited for hours without success. When we did get a ride, it was usually in the back of a pickup truck, and we quickly became covered with dust or mud from the unpaved roads. Sometimes we walked to the sub-district headquarters and tried to talk our way onto a government vehicle going to Wewak. This was always a problem. Technically, government vehicles were not permitted to carry "passengers", but in what was then a rather remote area without public transportation, rules were often ignored in favor of the public good, particularly when the driver or government officer was a "wantok", or person of the same linguistic or ethnic group. For this reason (among others), national officers were rarely posted to their home areas. Nevertheless, I was always grateful to the Patrol Officers and others who offered me rides and assistance during my earlier fieldwork, knowing that, without any resources of my own, I could not reciprocate.

I had left Neligum as an anthropologist without means, but I was returning as a government officer. What a difference! I had first arrived in Maprik, the sub-district headquarters closest to Neligum, covered with road dust and on foot, carrying only a backpack, exhausted from the long journey from Wewak that had taken several days. I had hitched rides in many different vehicles, and had slept in villages along the way. I didn't know anyone in Maprik, and had to ask directions to a small hotel. My return was a dramatic turnabout. The Administrative Officer at the Law Reform Commission had requisitioned a government Toyota Land Cruiser and driver for my personal use during this research trip. The driver had met me at the airstrip in Wewak and taken me to the nicest hotel in town (which I paid for with a government warrant). After a good night's sleep and a shower, he picked me up the next morning. I arrived in Maprik that afternoon, well rested and in clean clothes, and presented myself to the Deputy District Commissioner, the Officer in Charge of the station, whom I had known from my previous work. The trip to Neligum was equally painless. Some friends from Neligum had awaited my arrival in Maprik. The government driver took all of us to the end of the road, as far as the four-wheel-drive Toyota could travel. From there, we easily reached the village on foot after just a few hours.

My homecoming in Neligum was all that I had imagined. In 1974, a traditional leader, Moll Apulala (see Scaglion 2001; Scaglion and Norman 2000) had adopted me as his son. During my previous fieldwork, I had maintained a separate residence in a hamlet adjacent to his own, and had eaten meals with his family. Although I was not surprised, I was very pleased to learn that when the Village Court had been established for our area, Moll had been chosen as a Village Court Magistrate. He was a renowned mediator and accomplished at dispute settlement, so his selection made good sense. In further good luck for me, his fellow magistrates had chosen him as their leader, so he was now the Chairman of the Balupwine Village Court. I was delighted to know that we now had a professional relationship as well as a personal one, and that I would be assured of cooperation in the work I would be doing with the Village Court. I spent the weekend in Neligum with Moll and my Abelam family, renewing old acquaintances and visiting with friends. In an ironic twist, I was able to pay Moll for my accommodations with the extremely generous travel allowance with which government officers pay others (usually other government officers) when they stay in their homes when traveling in rural areas with no commercial accommodations.

This homecoming was the first of several returns I would make to Neligum during 1979–1981. My relationship with Moll, and with many others, was soon to take on a somewhat different character for several reasons. Before, I had been quite without resources and willing to share everything I had with my *wantoks*. But now, it seemed that my *wantoks* wanted me to share resources that I could sometimes command, but which I did not really control. One example was the government vehicle. When I had been a powerless "villager" like everyone else in Neligum, I sought to convince government officers to give me rides. Now, as a government officer with business to conduct, I had lots of villagers asking me for rides all over the district, and I simply could not honor all of their requests. Although I could have easily spent all of my time doing nothing but ferrying people to and fro, I always felt pangs of conscience whenever I had to refuse people. I felt less than human when, on official business, I had to pass people from Neligum, walking heavily laden, along the road. There were other aspects of my work that turned me into a person that I did not want to be. Before, as an anthropologist, I had had no pressing work schedule. I could wander around the village and opportunistically stop and chat with anyone and everyone who wanted to talk. Now I felt embarrassed when I was "too busy" to visit with old friends whom I had not seen in years, or to help people with their own projects, as I had always done so willingly before.

Another thing unsettled me. When I had been a "pure" anthropologist during the colonial era, and was accompanied by my Abelam friends, I often chose not to participate in the "European" world. When we went to Maprik together, for example, I did not accept the hospitality of Europeans unless my friends were also welcome. When my Abelam friends waited interminably outside government offices for an audience with the *kiap* or Patrol Officer, I waited with them, sitting on the grass with everyone else. I generally went to "native" establishments instead of "European" ones, because local people were often refused access to places catering to Europeans (the excuse usually being that they were not wearing shoes, not because they were "natives").

But now things were different. I had appointments with other government officers in Maprik, and I marched right in to see them—right past the throngs of people waiting outside for an audience—but I had to leave my friends behind. I no longer wore the *bilas* or distinctive clothing of the anthropologist—ratty shorts (stubbies), singlet (T-shirt) and thongs, but rather the *bilas* of the *kiap*—nicely pressed shorts, collared, epauletted shirt, long socks and proper leather tie shoes. I had lunches in clubs with my fellow officers—and again had to leave my Abelam friends behind. I often felt like a hypocrite.

My relationship with my Abelam father, Moll Apulala, took an unexpected turn. During my initial fieldwork, we were operating entirely in his world. He had been very much the teacher and I the student. He spent countless hours teaching me the language and culture of his people. At first he was very tolerant, but as my knowledge and skills increased, he became more impatient, because I was not progressing at a rate he considered acceptable. Still, he was always kind and considerate, always maintained his sense of humor, and we had a warm and mutually respectful relationship. That didn't change, fortunately. But now we were operating in my world as much as his, and I often found myself in the role of teacher. I took him into European settings, wearing shoes for the first time in his life (he hated them). I translated for him (he spoke no English, although I tried to teach him). I explained the culture of my people to him. He didn't progress at the rate I hoped, but I tried to be patient.

Our relative prestige suddenly seemed topsy-turvy. In the village, he was the big man, the traditional leader of our lineage, and I was just his often incompetent son. In town, however, I was the government legal officer, the Director of Customary Law for the Law Reform Commission, and senior to the Village Courts Officer in Maprik, his boss. I knew the law, I set up Village Courts, I supervised them. I knew how they should operate. I had become my father's boss. As a Village Court Magistrate, he had to account to me. And I really wanted to make some changes. That was my charge as a government officer.

Anthropologists normally take a detached, objective, observational posture. Often, they don't want to influence things too much, because they want to see how things operate under ordinary conditions. When I waited for hours with my Abelam friends for an audience with the *kiap*, I probably could have gotten them in to see him simply by going to talk with him myself and asking. But I had the time to wait, and part of my job was to see what happens to village people who go to see the *kiap* unaccompanied by a Westerner. As an anthropologist, I tended not to take much action—I would just "go with the flow". But as a government officer, I often felt as though I had to create the flow. There were problems with the national legal system, and I had been hired to help fix them. Back in Port Moresby, anthropologists had begun to frustrate me at times. When given concrete proposals for legal change, anthropologists were quick to point out potential problems, but were not equally quick with solutions. They knew what *not* to do, but seemed less interested in collaborating with me to determine what should be done.

More Problems in Port Moresby

Sometimes I turned the cautionary posture of anthropologists to my advantage. A draft "anti-excessive compensation" bill had been prepared, and I didn't like it. Compensation is a form of conflict management, common in Melanesian societies, in which an aggrieved party or parties demand payment of some sort from another party. The payment demanded is generally thought to be proportionate to the wrong, and is usually proportionate to the magnitude of the dispute as well. Payment of compensation ordinarily implies acceptance of responsibility by the donors and willingness to terminate the dispute on the part of the recipients. Such arrangements, although very common in Melanesian customary law, were not formally recognized under national law.

Recently, a series of popularized cases had uncovered a problem with this customary law practice. In one dispute, for example, a man from one province had been driving a vehicle that struck and killed a man from another province. The victim's clan was demanding hundreds of thousands of dollars in compensation from the whole of the driver's province. Clearly, homicide compensation appeared to be an area in which rapid social changes had outstripped the ability of small-scale customary legal systems to adapt. Inflationary compensation demands had diverted cash from development and created law and order problems in various areas of the country. How then could the customary law patterns be preserved but adapted to contemporary conditions?

The draft bill (Law Reform Commission 1980) formally recognized customary compensation as an institution for dispute resolution. It permitted exchanges of wealth and services for settling compensation demands for death, injuries, and property damage, and provided for appropriate tribunals to decide cases. But I felt that the bill was too "rule-oriented". It tried to control and regulate claims and payments by specifying circumstances and amounts for such payments, which I felt would destroy flexibility. Furthermore, it didn't seem to me as though the broader social milieu in which compensation payments operate was being considered adequately. So Rob Gordon (another anthropologist) and I rounded up some other anthropologists to prepare papers commenting on the bill from the viewpoint of their field sites (Scaglion 1981). True to form, the anthropologists identified particular geographical areas in which the bill would cause problems, and pointed out some of the possible unintended consequences of stipulating maximum payments. For example, Andrew Strathern (1981) showed how Hagen compensation payments were part of the escalating competitive exchange system called *moka*, and cautioned against setting limits on *moka* or confusing it with the compensation payments associated with it. This, I thought, was a real contribution, and resulted in some positive changes to the draft bill.

With all of these projects going on simultaneously: supervising the student researchers, liaising with the Village Courts Secretariat, conducting research in the Sepik, responding to the customary compensation draft bill, etc., the time passed very quickly. After a year had elapsed, I began to think about my return to the United States. It was already July 1980, and I had to get my family home by late August so that we could begin the new school year. I made a routine request for leave fares so that I could purchase tickets for our return journey, but I was in for a horrible shock. The Public Services Commission refused my request! It turned out that the agreement that I had made with the Law Reform Commission violated PSC guidelines. Contract officers had to work eighteen months (not fifteen) before they were eligible for leave fares. I quickly consulted with Justice Department lawyers. I had a formal contract with the Justice Department that stipulated the scheduling of my work. The contract had been approved by the PSC. Clearly, I was in the right. The Justice Department lawyers agreed to represent me, and to press my grievance with the PSC, but they warned that it probably would take much longer to settle the case than the one month I had remaining. Thus, my wife and I could not have gotten home in time to resume our teaching duties. Nor could I afford the nearly $8,000 it would have taken to purchase the fares pending an outcome of the case. I really felt trapped.

The way we finally worked out the problem was not at all to my liking, but I really had no choice. I had to "go finish", in local parlance. PSC guidelines permit the early termination of an officer's contract by mutual consent, so I had to agree. The Law Reform Commission offered to hire me again as a consultant according to the schedule, salary, and terms we had set for my original contract, but there were several major problems with this offer. First, consultants were not issued with government houses as were contract officers, so I would have to give up my hard-won house. Second, dependents were not supported for consultants, and I did not fancy returning to Papua New Guinea for nine months without my family. Third and most important, a nine-month consultancy period was not permitted under PSC guidelines. So I left Papua New Guinea without any sort of return contract, because we could not work out the details before I had to depart.

Some Accomplishments

Back in the United States, I had no major problems reconciling my work for the Law Reform Commission with my work as an Assistant Professor of Anthropology. Academic positions carry with them the expectation of engaging in research, and it was no problem to accomplish the work I had to do. The student researchers had gathered some 600 extended cases from all over the country. I devised a coding scheme to identify salient variables of cases, such as type of case, geographical area, remedy agents used, and decision reached. I supervised the coding of cases, and completed a basic computer analysis of them. I wrote a computer retrieval system to make them accessible for legal researchers. I was able to efficiently supervise my full-time project officer, Bospidik Pilokos, in Port Moresby, consulting with her in pre-arranged monthly phone calls.

What I was not able to do efficiently was to negotiate my return contract as a consultant. If I thought it was a herculean task to be allocated a government house, this was worse. I just could not get action. I must have spent nearly as much in phone calls as I hoped to make in salary. If I had not invested so much time and energy in my project, I surely would have abandoned the effort. Finally my monumental struggles were rewarded, and I managed to arrange for a three-month contract to return as a consultant during June to August in 1981. In another major victory, I was awarded a work visa that extended through August 1982, so that I could return the next (North American) summer without having to reapply for a visa. Things were looking up. I assured my university that I would be back to teach the full academic year from September to April in 1981–1982, and set out for Papua New Guinea once again.

In May 1981, I arrived triumphantly on the tarmac at Jackson's Airport in Port Moresby. As I exited the plane, I waved to my friend Ross DeVere, Principal Legal Officer for the Law Reform Commission, who had come to pick me up. I felt like kissing the ground. Apart from genuinely loving Papua New Guinea, I had labored so hard to have the opportunity to complete some of my research, I felt quite relieved. I got right to work. I organized all of the extended cases in Law Reform Commission files, and began to consult with lawyers who wanted to use the cases as precedents to argue customary law in court. I began to edit the second monograph (Scaglion 1983) in the Law Reform Commission Monographs Series I had initiated. I again worked with the Village Courts Secretariat to complete some of our projects. I really wanted to wrap up loose ends, because I was not at all sure that I would be returning again in this capacity. Some of my other undertakings are described in Scaglion (1987).

When I left Papua New Guinea in August 1981, I assured officers of the Law Reform Commission of my desire to continue the work the following summer. There was still a lot to do, including the construction of draft bills. But I was candid in telling them that I could not invest the effort that

I had the previous year in arranging for a contract. If I received a contract, I would happily return in May 1982. But I wasn't hopeful. During the intervening academic year, I continued to work on Law Reform Commission projects (e.g. Scaglion and Whittingham 1985), but sure enough, the summer of 1982 passed without a contract. Once again, I was a "pure" anthropologist.

The Aftermath

I was granted a sabbatical leave from the University of Pittsburgh beginning in January 1983, and decided to return to Papua New Guinea as an anthropologist. I offered my services for free to the Law Reform Commission, and was able to complete some unfinished business, but my days as a government officer were over. I left Port Moresby destined for the peace and quiet of Neligum. In April 1983 I arrived in Maprik covered with road dust and on foot, carrying only a backpack, exhausted from the long journey from Wewak that had taken several days. I had hitched rides in many different vehicles, and had slept in villages along the way. I was again wearing the uniform of the anthropologist: short pants, singlet, and thongs. As Yogi Berra once said, "It was déjà vu all over again".

Actually, it wasn't so bad, to be "powerless" again. I had become really frustrated with a bureaucracy that seemed determined to undermine my best efforts to accomplish what I had been hired to do. The demands of the job had never sat very well on me in the Sepik in any case, and I was happy once again to return to village life—to have the time to talk to people, to share what little I had, and to be grateful once again for the hospitality of my friends.

My work as a government officer was to have some lasting effects on my relationship with the people of Neligum village, however. In Port Moresby, I always seemed to be arguing the cause of ordinary villagers, who rarely have advocates, before an inflexible and sometimes uncaring bureaucracy. Yet as a government officer among the Abelam, I felt acutely that I was part of that bureaucracy. In some of the ethnical dilemmas described earlier, my government duties had conflicted with my responsibilities as a member of the local community. During my first visit to Neligum, I had shared in village life as completely as possible, given that I was an outsider. As a government officer, I could not. In many Abelam eyes (and my own), I had been revealed as a Westerner first and a community member second. My incorporation into Neligum society had been interrupted, and I was never able to regain the momentum I had once enjoyed. I had been caught between two worlds.

Acknowledgments

I am grateful to the Government of Papua New Guinea for permission to conduct my research there, and to the funding agencies that have supported my efforts. I owe a particular debt to the people of Neligum Village for their exceptional hospitality, generosity, and continuing tolerance of me and my work throughout the years. The friends and colleagues who have provided assistance are too numerous to mention, but their help has been critical to my endeavors.

References

Fitzpatrick, P. 1980 *Law and State in Papua New Guinea*. New York: Academic Press.

Galanter, M. 1981 "Justice in Many Rooms: Courts, Private Ordering and Indigenous Law". *Journal of Legal Pluralism* 19:1–47.

Gordon, R. and M. Meggitt 1985 *Law and Order in the New Guinea Highlands: Encounters with Enga*, New Hanover: University Press of New England.

Grimes, B.F. (ed) 1992 *Ethnologue: Languages of the World* (12th edition). Dallas: Summer Institute of Linguistics.

Law Reform Commission of Papua New Guinea 1980 "Customary Compensation". Report no. 11. Port Moresby: PNG Government Printers.

Nader, L. and H. F. Todd, Jr. 1978 *The Disputing Process: Law in Ten Societies*. New York: Columbia University Press

Pospisil, L. 1971 *Anthropology of Law: A Comparative Theory*, New York: Harper and Row.

Paliwala, A. 1982 "Law and Order in the Village: The Village Courts". In D. Weisbrot, A. Paliwala, and A. Sawyerr (eds) *Law and Social Change in Papua New Guinea*, pp. 191–217. Sydney: Butterworths.

Paliwala, A. and D. Weisbrot 1982 "Changing Society through Law: An Introduction". In D. Weisbrot, A. Paliwala, and A. Sawyerr (eds) *Law and Social Change in Papua New Guinea*, pp. 3–12. Sydney: Butterworths.

Scaglion, R. 1976 "Seasonal Patterns in Western Abelam Conflict Management Practices". Ph.D. diss., University of Pittsburgh.

———— 1979 "Formal and Informal Operations of a Village Court in Maprik". *Melanesian Law Journal* 7:116–129.

———— 1987 "Customary Law Development in Papua New Guinea". In R.M. Wulff and S. Fiske (eds) *Anthropological Praxis: Translating Knowledge into Action*, pp. 98–108. Boulder: Westview Press.

———— 1990 "Legal Adaptation in a Papua New Guinea Village Court". *Ethnology* 29:17–33.

———— 2001 "Juxtaposed Narratives: A New Guinea Big Man Encounters the Colonial Process". In N. McPherson (ed) *Colonial New Guinea: Anthropological Perspectives*. ASAO Monograph Series No. 19. Pittsburgh: University of Pittsburgh Press.

———— (ed) 1981 *Homicide Compensation in Papua New Guinea: Problems and Prospects*. Law Reform Commission of Papua New Guinea, Monograph No. 1. Port Moresby: Office of Information.

———— 1983 *Customary Law in Papua New Guinea: A Melanesian View*. Law Reform Commission of Papua New Guinea, Monograph No. 2. Port Moresby: PNG Government Printer.

Scaglion, R. and M. Norman 2000 "Where Resistance Falls Short: Rethinking Agency through Biography". In P.J. Stewart and A. Strathern (eds) *Identity Work: Constructing Pacific Lives*, pp. 121–138. ASAO Monograph Series No. 18. Pittsburgh: University of Pittsburgh Press,

Scaglion, R. and R. Whittingham 1985 "Female Plaintiffs and Sex-Related Disputes in Rural Papua New Guinea". In S. Toft (ed) *Domestic Violence in Papua New Guinea*, pp. 120–133. Law Reform Commission Monograph No. 3. Port Moresby

Strathern, A.J. 1981 "Compensation: Should There be a New Law?" In R. Scaglion (ed) *Homicide Compensation in Papua New Guinea: Problems and Prospects*, pp. 5–24. Port Moresby: Office of Information.

———— 1984 *A Line of Power*. New York: Tavistock.

Strathern, M. 1972 *Official and Unofficial Courts: Legal Assumptions and Expectations in a Highlands Community*. Canberra: New Guinea Research Unit Bulletin No. 47.

Westermark, G. 1978 "Village Courts in Question: The Nature of Court Procedure". *Melanesian Law Journal* 6:79–96.

———— 1981 "Legal Pluralism and Village Courts in Agarabi". Ph.D. diss., University of Washington.

Chapter 3

Environmental Non-Governmental Organizations and the Nature of Ethnographic Inquiry

Paige West

Introduction

Non-governmental organizations (NGOs) have become an important part of anthropological inquiry and practice. We analyze them, critique them, and work with them. In addition, some NGOs now provide waged labor—as consultants and long-term employees—for anthropologists. In many instances NGOs have become the discursive and material terrain through which people living in "out-of-the-way" places (Tsing 1993:10), the traditional subjects of anthropological/ethnographic research, are known by outsiders and managed by state-like entities. While it has been argued that NGOs are an extension of civil society and the public will (Wapner 1996), they are also bureaucratic apparatuses which produce, circulate, and then act upon particular discourses about people, nature, and culture.[1] Subjects that were, in the past, the domain of anthropological/ethnographic inquiry. With these discourses, NGOs set the tone regarding many social issues, frame public action, and garner public support (Weeks 1999:19).

    In this essay I argue that NGO discourses about people, nature, and culture have changed the nature of anthropological and ethnographic inquiry in situations in which we work with and for NGOs, and in situations where we merely work in the same physical spaces as NGOs. My arguments are focused upon environmentally concerned NGOs and discourses about the relationship between culture (the social practices of people) and nature (biological diversity). I agree with Brosius when he argues that environmentally focused discourses come to constitute reality and that they, "in their constitutiveness define various forms of agency, administer certain

Notes for this chapter begin on page 83.

silences, and prescribe various forms of intervention" (Brosius 1999:277–278). Using ethnographic examples from my work in Papua New Guinea's Crater Mountain Wildlife Management Area, an area which is part of an NGO managed integrated environmental conservation and economic development project, I examine how the co-opting of the traditional subjects of anthropological inquiry by NGOs and their incorporation into NGO discourse changes the nature of anthropological research.

Integrated Conservation and Development Projects

In the past, national parks and wildlife reserves were the methods used by environmental NGOs in their efforts to conserve biological diversity.[2] These interventions were based on models derived from conservation interventions in the United States dating from the turn of the nineteenth century (Hecht and Cockburn 1990). This transportation of the American generated "national park" model for conservation abroad came under international scrutiny in the early 1980s. Conservationists argued that national park-like interventions were not successful because the people living on the edges of the protected areas did not recognize their boundaries when conducting their traditional subsistence practices (Brown and Wyckoff-Baird 1992; Wells and Brandon 1992: ix).

One of the responses to this criticism of international environmental conservation projects was the development of the "integrated conservation and development project (ICAD or ICDP)". This model, although it existed in practice earlier (Bonner 1994:253–270), has been used widely since the early 1990s (Wells, Brandon, and Hannah 1992).[3] With this model, conservation NGOs began to incorporate the language of "local participation" into their rhetoric, arguing that people living adjacent to protected areas used the resources they were trying to protect and that if they were provided with an alternative source of income conservation interventions would be more successful. Conservationists came to the conclusion that for NGOs to meet their mandate of conserving biological diversity they must incorporate local "social and economic development" into their conservation projects (Brandon and Wells 1992:557). Schroeder has called this reliance by environmentalist on "positive economic incentives to promote sound land use practices" the "commodity road to stabilization" and critiqued the use of capital intensive strategies as a tool for environmental preservation or stabilization (Schroeder 1995:326).[4] Even with this inherent contradiction, integrated conservation and development projects became entrenched in the conservation and development bureaucracy.

The fundamental premise of these projects is that local development should take a backseat to the conservation of biodiversity and the strengthening of protected areas. Providing economic development options for local people is a means toward the end of biodiversity conservation and not an end in itself. Early ICAD practitioners recognized that making the link between conservation and development through the further introduction of capitalist institutions into village life was almost impossible (Wells, Brandon, and Hannah 1992:xi). Yet, this method for the design and implementation of conservation projects has been used worldwide. These projects generally rely on extractive reserves, eco-tourism, non-timber forest products, green marketing, and adventure tourism as the conduits for the capitalization of village life.

In much of the literature associated with ICADs local people are discursively constructed as a "threat" to the biological diversity of their lands. At their base, ICADs are about changing the actions and practices of local people in order to meet the end goal of conservation. More specifically, they are about the integration of local peoples into commodity based systems of production as a strategy for the conservation of biological diversity. Local historic subsistence practices are curtailed so that the local people, who through these practices were seen as a threat to biodiversity, can engage in economic and subsistence practices sanctioned by conservation biologists and development practitioners as environmentally appropriate. In lieu of the language of exclusion used in previous models for conservation, the conservation rhetoric now incorporates development discourses as the central method for achieving biodiversity conservation globally (Sachs 1993). This change in language and thought places the traditional subjects of anthropological inquiry—"local people"—directly into the intellectual, discursive, and material terrain of conservation biologists and environmentally focused NGOs.

The Crater Mountain Wildlife Management Area

Papua New Guinea's Crater Mountain Wildlife Management Area is the product of a long series of local, national, and transnational exchanges between individuals and institutions (West 2000). The project began in the late 1970s with the work of an Australian photographer. During his work in PNG he became fascinated with Birds of Paradise and concerned that local people were not conserving them. During the 1980s he raised interest among international conservation NGOs in the conservation of Bird of Paradise habitat near Ubaigubi, Herowana, Haia, and Maimafu villages. The land held by families in these four villages' crosses the boundaries of the Eastern Highlands Province, the Gulf Province, and the Chimbu Province. The ethnographic examples in this essay are drawn from my work with people who speak a sub-dialect of the Gimi language and who live in Maimafu Village.[5]

The Crater Mountain Wildlife Management Area (WMA) was officially established in 1994. The Papua New Guinea Department of Environment and Conservation (DEC) declared it a national Wildlife Management Area under the Faunal (Protection and Control) Act of 1976. The Act establishes the mechanisms by which "Wildlife Management Areas, Sanctuaries, and Protected Areas" are set up and maintained. The Act provides for a set of formal institutionalized mechanisms to regulate wildlife harvesting, possession, and trade in these areas. The Act does not regulate land use or management.

The Research and Conservation Foundation of Papua New Guinea (RCF), an NGO established in 1986, administers the Crater Mountain project. RCF has attempted to meet their conservation and development goals by implementing a series of programs within the four villages located in the WMA. These programs include: creating local businesses revolving around biological research, tourism, and handicraft production; training local men to work with biologists; teaching local men and children about biological diversity and conservation; and implementing a monitoring system to measure the results of biodiversity conservation. RCF was begun specifically to manage the Crater Mountain project and has been funded by both The Wildlife Conservation Society (WCS) and The Biodiversity Conservation Network (BCN).

WCS was founded in New York in 1859 as the New York Zoological Society. It began as a local non-profit organization for the protection and maintenance of The New York Zoological Park Bronx Zoo and for the encouragement of scientific research and, in particular, zoological research. Since its inception WCS has sponsored field research and began to sponsor the protection of parks and protected areas all over the world in 1907. To date the NGO conducted over 270 projects in over 50 countries, including the United States. The WCS International Conservation Program carries out conservation interventions undertaken in international sites and their Asia Program carries out the work sponsored in Papua New Guinea.

BCN was the major donor for the Crater Mountain project and RCF during the period of fieldwork I discuss in this chapter. BCN was designed to fund and study international conservation projects that linked biological conservation with economic development and was based upon the ideologies and practices of the aforementioned ICAD project analysis from the early 1990s. The ideology behind BCN, that biodiversity is inextricably linked to capital and nature, is discussed in BCN literature as "biological capital". Local communities are at the base of the BCN program: "Conservation efforts that ignore the economic needs of local communities are unlikely to succeed. The Biodiversity Conservation Network (BCN), a component of the Biodiversity Support Program (BSP), is an innovative USAID-funded program working in the Asia/Pacific Region to provide grants for community-based enterprises that directly depend on biodiversity" (BCN 1997: iii). BCN takes as its premise that commodity production and economic incentives which tie local people to commodity based systems are the strategies that will promote the conservation of biological diversity. The BCN project began in earnest with a 20 million-dollar commitment from USAID in 1992 and was planned to last for six and a half years ending in March 1999.[6]

In the ethnographic examples that follow I demonstrate the social and material effects of the NGO generated discourse about nature and culture relating to the local people living within the bounds of the Crater Mountain Wildlife Management Area. During my fieldwork in 1996–1998, the ways in which these NGOs created, held, and acted upon images forced me to do "salvage ethnography" in order to counter them. My initial fieldwork plan did not include the collection of data about "the Gimi" as a social or cultural group. Indeed, my project was framed in terms of the analysis of the social relations between project participants—both Gimi speakers and conservation biologists—as a new kind of social group particular to the global environmental relations of late modernity. However, the constant and overwhelming production of Gimi speakers and their subsistence and social practices as threats to the environment, and the conservationists co-opting of anthropological terms as a shorthand explanation for local social practices, prompted me to conduct particular ethnographic research in order to counter these discourses. These NGO generated discourses changed the nature of my anthropological inquiry. While I did collect the data I initially set out to gather—data on the social history of the Crater Mountain project and the social relations between its participants—I also collected data on very traditional anthropological topics such as socio-political organization, subsistence practices, land tenure, and the loss of tradition and the invention of tradition. I collected this data in order to critique the pervasive discursive production of "the Gimi culture" created by NGOs.[7]

Producing the Gimi I: Co-opting Anthropological Terms

The Crater Mountain Wildlife Management Area covers two language groups, Gimi and Pawaians [*sic*]. The Gimi population is bigger than the Pawaiian with the Pawaians population numbering somewhere in excess of 600, while we calculate that the Gimi living within or about the northern borders of Crater probably reach four times that number. The Gimi villages of Crater are traditional Highland 'Bigman' societies. Each clan has one or more 'Bigmen' (chiefs) who maintain their position through their skill as politicians or fight leaders. The Gimi are subsistence farmers who follow shifting agriculture or swidden farming patterns.

The criteria for maintaining status as a Bigman in present day Crater Society is evolving constantly, the Gimi sections of Crater in particular are in the process of rapid social change. In the past Bigmen would have achieved their power through political skills or their ability to lead as a warrior. To this list one must now add the role of the businessman, parliamentarian, or government bureaucrat. The Macks report that Pawaians in Haia have maintained their traditional living patterns to a higher degree than have the Gimi. (RCF/WCS 13:1995)

In most publications about the Crater Mountain project by NGOs, the same images of Gimi speakers are produced in each article (BCN 1996, 1997, 1998, 2000; Johnson 1997; Pearl 1994; WCS 1995). Gimi speaking peoples living in three distinct villages and speaking three dialects of the Western dialect of Gimi, in approximately two paragraphs in each publication, are described as big man societies, shifting or swidden agriculturists, and people whose subsistence practices threaten their ancestral forests. Population estimates for Gimi speakers living in the Crater Mountain Wildlife Management Area are also given. The constant reproduction of these factors is significant.

In each of these publications thousands of individuals are described in a few paragraphs. The paragraphs that are dedicated to cultural background information invariably are insignificant compared to other sections such as: site background, project goals, objectives, activities, and outputs, baseline geographic information, biological significance of the area, endangered and threatened species, economically and culturally valuable species, and threats to biodiversity. The people who hold the land that is being discussed as highly biologically diverse, under threat, and in need of conservation are relegated to space in the publications after descriptions of plants and animals. The people and their cultural practices are clearly of secondary importance.

While the designation "big man society" is useful in anthropological explanations, its deployment as a short hand way of describing all of the social relations within a society is problematic. Traditionally, anthropologists have argued that this type of sociopolitical organization is an elaborated version of the village headman system. Big men have social and political power because of their generosity, fitness, bravery, eloquence, wealth, ability to navigate government bureaucracies, past travel to other places, and so on. Big men are also big men because of their support in villages other than their village of residence. This system ties people regionally and creates connections among villages. Furthermore, big men societies are almost always associated with complex systems of horticulture and exchange. Finally, big men are not "chiefs", as "chiefs" are political leaders in chiefdoms, which are a completely different form of sociopolitical organization.

People in Maimafu do indeed exhibit some of the cultural characteristics associated with big man societies in the anthropological literature. The problem with the NGO publications is that they never describe those characteristics. The same is the case with the references to agricultural practices. Saying that "the Gimi" are "shifting or swidden agriculturists" does not supply any information about how people garden, what they grow, how they choose land for new gardens, or the social relations involved in horticultural practices. Nor does it exhibit any knowledge about the differences, much discussed in the anthropological literature, between agriculture and horticulture. My data suggests that people living in Maimafu village are horticulturists who predominately cut tertiary and secondary growth when preparing new gardens. The lack of attention paid by environmental conservationists to local horticultural practices is troubling. Much of their rhetoric concerning local people as threats to the environment is based on how people use their land and population. Both of these issues are intimately tied to subsistence practices. There are marked differences between horticulture, agriculture, and swidden agriculture.

The NGO obsession with land use and population is important for many reasons. Biologists working on this project often argue that local population growth puts too much pressure on local biological diversity and that population control measures should be put into place in the villages. This focus on population is part of a wider tendency to discursively produce local people as threats to the environment. The focus on land use and tenure is part of the same tendency. The NGO fixation on land ownership and tenure is tied to the desire to wrest the control of this land from its holders. In NGO publications and in conversations with conservation practitioners, land relations are boiled down to questions of "who owns the land?" This simplification of genealogical and historic land use practices demonstrates, again, the lack of understanding of local sociality and local cultural configurations.

Property rights and land tenure have been the subject of some of the most complex and contested debates in anthropology (see McCay and Acheson 1990). In Melanesia, the relationship between "social space and environmental place is particularly rich and important" (Knauft 1999:222; see also Morren 1986; Rappaport 1984; Wagner 1972). This relationship between people and place is tied to questions of identity, group affiliation, changes in the landscape, changes in external sites of power, commodification of resources, and "development" in general (Bennett 1995; Filer 1990; Hyndman 1994; Knauft 1999:223). Local representations of property relations can never be taken simply as "true" statements about the world. Blinkoff (n.d.:11) uses the word "portrayals" to describe such representations among the Sokamin; "layers upon layers of portrayals exist. Privilege one layer and you mask or delegitimize another. Try to blend layers and you lose complexity".

Generalizations about property relations are therefore problematic in this context. Property relations and practices in Maimafu are dynamic and vary along historical, social, economic, and political dimensions. Land tenure is also intimately tied to the genealogical system in the village.

In Maimafu, different kinds of rights to, and relationships with, different kinds of land are held at multiple levels within the community and decisions about land usage are very rarely made entirely by individuals. While individual choices are sanctioned or not sanctioned by the community, these choices are made in accordance with a number of different kinds of valid claims to land, which are made on the basis of: kinship or lineality, previous use or the history of use, the history of social relations, exchange or gift relations, mythological "charters", current social situations, current political situations, current economic situations, and current individual and group interests. Claims made on these diverse grounds are all possibly valid, and different claims made on different grounds made by different groups or individuals about the same tract of land are common. In addition, these grounds have changed over time.

In using these anthropologically generated terms for social and subsistence practices in a way that demonstrates an almost total disregard for the anthropological literature, conservationists are limiting the ability of those reading their publications to understand life in the rural villages involved in the Crater Mountain project. They are also limiting their own ability to understand local environmental uses. I would like to say that these anthropological terms are employed in order to succinctly describe the people involved in the project, but that is not the case. Not one of the biologists working in the Crater Mountain Wildlife Management Area reported having read the ethnographic literature about "the Gimi".[8] Nor did they demonstrate any complex knowledge about local political systems, local gardening practices, or local property relations, the very subjects that speak directly to local uses of the environment. Rather, the conservation practitioners who designed and managed the Crater Mountain project used anecdotal information provided by biologists and conservationists not good social scientific data and explanations, as their primary source for understanding of local social and subsistence practices.[9]

Michael Taussig (1987:27), in a discussion about the inscription of colonial ideas on the bodies of native South Americans argues: "Perhaps, as in the manner strenuously theorized by Michel Foucault in his work on discipline, what was paramount here was the inscription of a mythology in the Indian body, an engraving of civilization locked in struggle with wildness whose model was taken from the colonists' fantasies about Indian cannibalism". Just as the body of the Indian became a site for the collapsing of violence, ideology, power, knowledge, economy, force, and discourse (Taussig 1987:29), the bodies of villagers from Maimafu have become sites for the collapsing of conservationists notions of Giminess and indigenousness. These notions, while described using the language of anthropology are not based in any understanding of the anthropological literature. These narratives become a reality and they become the filters through which future actions and practices are carried out.

Producing the Gimi II: The Descent of the True Primitive

Gimi culture, before decontrol in the early 1960s, was a rich and exotic fusion of ritual, myth and bush knowledge built upon the experiences of countless generations living in Crater forests. As was often the case elsewhere administrators and missionaries working in the northern regions of the Gimi language area have been the perpetrators of massive cultural change. Many Gimi now believe that it is sinful to participate in or to be allied with the traditional rites of initiation and marriage. Gimi Christians consider the theater associated with these rites to border on evil. The culture that existed before Western penetration of Crater fathered a land philosophy of unexpected power and beauty. In the last ten years most ritual culture has disappeared. (RCF/WCS 1995:14)

One hot afternoon during my fieldwork I had a conversation with a conservation practitioner visiting Maimafu. While walking along a mountain trail past bamboo houses and vegetable gardens he said, "The Gimi in Maimafu are so acculturated that it's like they are not even real Gimi". We had been discussing the role of the Seventh-day Adventist Church in the community, and he had wanted to know what effects I thought that it had on local hunting practices. His sentiment that the people living in Maimafu are somehow less "Gimi" than other people because of their current daily social practices and beliefs is important. The idea that indigenous peoples are fixed sets of communities that somehow lose their authenticity when they stop practicing particular sets of behaviors, indicates a lack of understanding of the history of change over time in human societies. Anthropologists have written widely about this tendency, even within certain schools of anthropology, often debunking myths of "true primitives" and of seemingly isolated groups being a "window to our evolutionary past". Anthropologists have also written about the created exoticness of indigenous peoples by outsiders (see Kahn 2000).

Almost all of the conservation practitioners and tourists who visited Maimafu voiced disappointment when they found out that there are few local ritual practices tied to mythology, no initiation rituals, and little traditional dress. The "loss" of these imagined markers of indigenousness was seen as tragic. One tourist, disappointed when he realized that everyone in Maimafu wore second hand clothing from Australia, voiced his opinion by saying, "I guess I just thought that it would be more like those that the Discovery Channel shows and National Geographic". His comments reflect a media saturate image of what indigenous New Guineans are supposed to look and act like.[10] New Guinea and its inhabitants are produced as exotic and colorful. The television invites the viewer to gaze upon people that are visually other. The tourist and the conservation practitioner mark looks and acts as indicators of true indigenousness.

On another occasion, while voicing frustration with the property disputes in Maimafu, a conservation practitioner said, "It's not like they do anything else in the traditional way. Why do they have to be so damn picky about this?" His remark was answered with the following remark: "They just do it because they can. They do it because they want to screw up other people's chances of getting something they aren't going to get". Conservationists see the residents of Maimafu as employing traditional cultural structures and practices only when they are to their advantage. Of course, people's picking and choosing which customs to evoke at a particular time has been documented widely in Melanesia and is a kind of cultural practice in itself.

Much anthropological work has highlighted the production of tradition in Melanesia (Feinberg 1995; Hobsbawm and Ranger 1983; Jolly and Thomas 1992; Keesing and Tonkinson 1982; Lindstrom and White 1995; Linnekin 1992; White and Lindstrom 1993). Popular productions of culture constitute a valid area of inquiry for anthropologists (Lindstrom and White 1995:201). They are examples of local people working to make sense of modernization through existing cultural categories and that work, in turn, altering the categories through which development is processed. These productions of culture are contingent and political. They are sometimes the active attempt by local people to make political statements or to gain access to arenas of power (Lindstrom and White 1995). They highlight the fact that "concepts of (native) tradition and (European) modernity surround most fieldwork transactions" and they allow us to see the working out of the tensions between modernity and the traditional (Lindstrom and White 1995:204). Linnekin (1992) reviews much of this literature and problematizes the role of anthropologists in the "deconstruction" of local cultural forms. She highlights the political dilemmas associated with talking about cultural construction in the Pacific, questions the motives and desires of those who are "theorizing" the construction of culture, and calls for anthropologist to be careful when talking about authenticity. The choice on the part of the conservation practitioners to see one kind of tradition as essential to "Giminess" and another as a choice about behavior is tied to the anthropologically debunked notion of people without history (Wolf 1978).

Gimi speaking peoples are seen as more "Gimi-like" if they practice the traditions that are associated with them in the imaginations of the conservationists. They are seen as less "Gimi-like" if they do not. This form of essentializing creates a space where people in Maimafu and their cultural practices are seen as having less value than other people and other cultural practices. This imagination of an essential "Giminess" causes conservation practitioners to question social and subsistence rights of people living in Maimafu because they do not fit into this imaginary. This lack of essentialized traditional practices is used as one argument for wresting the control of land from these people. While the "Gimi" of the past had "a land philosophy of unexpected power and beauty" (RCF/WCS 1995:14), the people in Maimafu, because of their "acculturation", are seen as "threats" to the land. Their behaviors, which are not seen as sufficiently traditional, are seen as problems and "threats to biodiversity". A discourse has emerged in which it is argued that if local people alter their traditional practices and beliefs then they are not really authentic and therefore forfeit their rights to stewardship over their ancestral lands.

NGO Rhetorical Devices I: Paternity and Cargo

The people here, in Maimafu, Herowana, Ubaigubi, and Haia, are simple. They are uneducated. They do not know things about the environment like we do. They do not understand what they have here. They do not understand the value of their land. They are very simple people. We come here to teach them. We come here because we have the knowledge about how they can make their way in the world.

Let me tell you a story. In pidgin we call it a *tok picsa* (talk picture). I like to use these examples with villagers because they are easy for them to understand.

Suppose that I was your father and you were my son. I would take you and help you learn all that you need to know to make your way in the world. I would teach you how to hunt. I would teach you about being a man in our village. We would talk about the world and I would show you the way. I would not let you hunt alone at first. I would not let you stand up and speak to the other men at first. I would help you along the way. I would make you strong with my knowledge and then I would let you be your own man.

RCF is the father and Maimafu, Herowana, Ubaigubi, and Haia are our sons. But remember that the father looks after his children until they are independent. RCF has been finding food for its children. Scientists are part of that food. Tourists are part of that food. Now we must look for more food. But the villages, they are children still. They are not ready to go out and get their own food. (RCF employee, 1997)

When conservationists talk about the people living in the Crater Mountain Wildlife Management Area the image of local people as the children and of RCF as a parent is often evoked. Local people are discursively produced as too childish in their understandings of conservation and as "not ready yet" for access to development. The use of this metaphor is tied to a pervasive image of the people living in these rural villages as simple and childlike.

Over the course of my fieldwork I documented this metaphor being used when people from Maimafu fought over property relations, argued with conservation biologists, tried to communicate with a mining company, attempted to gain employment in the RCF office, and made demands about their development needs. It was used whenever people tried to gain power in their relationship with RCF. These discursive productions are a form of infantilizing paternalism in which indigenous people are seen as climbing an educational ladder toward modern industrial capitalism.

The other metaphor that is used often by RCF employees and conservation practitioners is that of a "cargo cult mentality". At one meeting between NGO employees and local people a young man stood up and made the following statement:

What we do not see here is the true hand mark of RCF. We see that you are here, we see that you are getting things from us, but what we do not see are the things that we need. We do not see medicine. We do not see a water supply. We do not see goods that we need. We do not see a source of meat for our children. Now let me make a talk picture for you. All of these things that you say that you have given us are little things.

This speech, which is about the lack of return that people in Maimafu feel with regard to their investments in conservation, was met with the following comment from the RCF employee running the discussion, "You people are just hungry for cargo. You have a cargo mentality where you think we should give you things and that you should not have to work for them".

The above commentary by the young man from Maimafu is a well put together critique of RCF. He is showing that people are willing to work hard for what they get and that they understand that when they work hard they deserve some return. He is saying that they, as a community, do not feel that they are currently getting the return that they were promised. The RCF employee, instead of addressing these issues, immediately draws upon the trope of "cargo". With this, he implies that people from Maimafu do not want to work but rather that they think that they deserve material wealth to magically and mysteriously come to them.

Cargo cults or millenarian movements can be seen as early examples of local attempts to understand and take part in the articulations between modernity, capitalism, and development. These socio-political religious and economic movements are one of the most creative articulations between the traditional and the modern (Kaplan 1995). Anthropologists have theorized them as some of the first local pushes for development (Whitehouse 1995). The language of cargo cults comes from anthropology. Early anthropologists such as F. E. Williams and Margaret Mead engaged these issues in their analyses of external influences on village life and the role of these influences in cultural change (Mead 1956, cited in Worsley 1968).

The anthropological literature on these movements shows that they were points where local people tried to work out the relationship between modernity and capitalism. The cargo cults were political and religious, secular and spiritual, and a creative reworking of modernity (Pred and Watts 1992). Mead's work demonstrates that these movements emphasized social improvement, economic improvement, political integration, and spiritual salvation. This is one of the things that makes these movements so interesting: they were in almost every sense very early development projects, and in fact, they were the first participatory development projects but since they were instigated, controlled, and organized by local people, the colonial government felt threatened by them (Mead 1956:208, cited in Worsley 1968). They were avenues for capitalism that were belittled by the colonial government precisely because they were generated from the periphery and not the center.

These movements were local cultural articulations that were used in attempts to access desirable material culture. They were attempts to use already existing cultural practices to access these new material commodities and, more broadly, development. They were local calls for modernization, and these calls were made through cultural categories constructed out of tradition, Christianity, and growing cultures of consumption. They were socio-political movements with specific historical backgrounds that show, when analyzed well, the intersection of capitalism, religion, politics, and desire (Kaplan 1995). They allowed Melanesians to work out feelings of insecurity and fear in the face of massive social change, brought about by interfaces with modernity, and to understand the economic changes that were taking place all around them, and they were also ways that local groups asserted independence or resistance (Worsley 1968:221).

Dismissing the development needs of Maimafu village by referring to local desires as a "cargo" mentality is an exercise in power. The local critiques of RCF have little to do with commodity goods and much to do with local attempts to gain access to services and cash earning possibilities. To say that the young man's speech was about "cargo" is to employ a convenient trope without addressing his critiques.

NGO Rhetorical Devices II: Threats to the Environment

Land use impacts on biodiversity include sago plantings, sweet potato garden plots, and the cutting of wood for fuel or local timber use. Hunting for subsistence and commercial purposes has already extirpated some species of game species in some regions of the WMA. Cuscus and tree kangaroo populations are seriously depleted. Cassowary populations are still strong, but the high rate of removal of cassowary chicks suggests a significant population crash might occur in a few years with the death of the existing adult populations [pers.com., Andrew Mack, 1995]. An increasing human population in the region will continue to have an escalating impact throughout the area. (Johnson 1997:369)

One afternoon my research assistants, Esta and Nara, and I were sitting in the front yard of my house when Nara said, "Do you have anything written by RCF about Maimafu?"[11] I went into the house and returned with the paper cited above (Johnson 1997). Nara began to read while Esta and I continued planning our upcoming trip to a mountain lake. After about an hour, Nara said, "Why do they never translate this kind of thing into Pidgin so that my father can read it? Or into our language?" I said that I did not know but that it might be fun to translate parts of it into Unavisa Gimi. We set out to do a translation experiment. Nara translated a few paragraphs into Unavisa Gimi and then gave them to Esta and she translated them back into English. "Land use impacts on biodiversity include sago plantings, sweet potato garden plots, and the cutting of wood for fuel or local timber use" when translated into Unavisa Gimi and then back translated becomes "The villagers use the forest. They have gardens with sago and sweet potatoes. They cut trees for firewood and trees to build houses".[12]

The tone of the original paper is one of indignation that local people use the forest. The paragraph is under the section heading "Threats to Biodiversity". When the paragraph was translated into Unavisa Gimi and then back into English that tone disappeared. The connotation of threats to the environment was gone. While there is the ability to express threat in Unavisa Gimi and people often do, there can be a threat of an impending fight or a person can threaten a mischievous cassowary, a person cannot threaten the forest. When we discussed the differences in the translations, both translators said that "it did not make sense" to talk about interactions with the forest in terms of threats because those interactions are necessary uses of the forest and land.

The paragraph from the Johnson article is an excellent example of the way that conservation practitioners discursively produced residents of Maimafu and their subsistence behaviors as "threats" to the environment. In all of these productions there is the over-arching image of human impact as unnatural and damaging. While the production of "threats" is prevalent in all published material there is little non-anecdotal data to back up these claims. To my knowledge, and confirmed by conversations with the scientific director of RCF and WCS biologists, when the Crater Mountain project began there had been no baseline study done to either document the level of biodiversity on lands held by people of Maimafu nor any baseline data collected about local land, animal, and forest use.

In the 1995 proposal given to BCN to garner funding for the ICAD project the NGO discusses human "threats" and "impacts" extensively in the early pages of the grant proposal. They go on, however, in pages 50–72 to propose a list of questions to be answered with the "monitoring component" of their project. These questions, to be asked and answered after the policies of conservation and development have already been implemented, include the collection of basic baseline data about human interactions with the environment, population, land use, hunting, other socially relevant behaviors, and studies of biological diversity in the area. The people are discursively produced as a threat before there is any data to indicate any sort of impact on their environment.

There are even predictions made about what will happen in the future based upon anecdotal evidence since no systematically collected data about any of these issues existed at the time that this proposal was written,

The growing number of residents concentrated around villages in the CMWMA will have a significant impact on wildlife populations in the near future. Before residents began congregating around the airstrip and the government sponsored facilities (aide post, school, DPI station), they roamed through the forest in small bands. Now that they are concentrated for long periods of time in the village, some sections of their forests are perhaps not hunted as heavily. Men from Heroana [sic], however, have been known to trespass on Pawaiian [sic] land and harvest wildlife using shotguns. This would further suggest that the land around Heroana is experiencing a shortage of game. Most grown men remember fondly early hunting trips with their fathers when they would return to the village from the forest with plenty of game. Today, when one sees village children eating meat, it is most likely wild rat. (RCF/WCS 1995:12)

People living in Maimafu, Herowana, and Ubaigubi are sedentary and have never "roamed through the forest in small bands" unless this refers to small male hunting parties. Since the context of the sentence is that of settlement patterns I assume it does not. Sedentary life does not mean that parts of the landscape which are held in tenure are not hunted simply because they are far away from villages (Morren 1986). In the above paragraph there is a correlation implied between the anecdotal evidence about men from Herowana "trespassing" on land held in tenure by people from Haia and the level of biodiversity or number of species on land held in tenure by people from Herowana. There is no evidence to back up this correlation and there are many other possible explanations.

The grant proposal goes on with this discussion of human "threats" to the biodiversity of the area,

Overhunting has already extirpated some game species in some regions of the WMA. Cuscus and tree kangaroo populations are seriously depleted. Cassowary populations are still strong, but the high rate of removal of cassowary chicks suggests a significant population crash might occur in a few years with the death of the existing adult populations. Overall, the threats to biodiversity are real and of major consequence, but they have not reached the critical point yet. With the implementation of improved land-use and extraction practices, biodiversity could be conserved in a substantially pristine condition. Delay of implementation of such practices will create a situation requiring efforts to bring about a recovery of biodiversity, a much more difficult and undesirable situation. (RCF/WCS 1995:12)

Again, there was no non-anecdotal data on populations of tree kangaroo or cuscus around Maimafu at the time that this proposal was written. The language used to describe what can happen if RCF/WCS is granted this money, "biodiversity could be conserved in a substantially pristine condition", indicates a true lack of understanding of land use patterns in the area and of the concept of landscape in general. The biodiversity that exists in and around Maimafu exists with the whole history of human use. The people of Maimafu, through the subsistence patterns the NGO wishes to curtail, produced the landscape in which they live. The absurdity of protecting biodiversity from the very people that through their tenure, hunting, gardening, and settlement actions produced the landscape is apparent. Indeed, if conservation in these terms were to "succeed" the practitioners would end up with a very different landscape than the one that they set out to conserve!

In these discursive productions of people as "threats" some of the actions attributed to the inhabitants of Maimafu, Herowana, and Ubaigubi are factually incorrect,

> It is still unclear how much biodiversity is lost following slash-and-burn and regrowth. It is abundantly clear, however, that the growing numbers of people will increase the impact on biodiversity due to excessive cutting for fuel wood and construction materials and damaged water quality by poor land-use near streams and poor sanitation. This impact will be compounded by a larger labor force looking to increase their incomes with larger coffee gardens. (RCF/WCS 1995:12)

None of these people practice "slash-and-burn" agriculture. They do not burn the forest. They clear secondary and tertiary growth with bush knives, weed garden plots by hand, and burn piles of brush.

This production of people as a threat is pervasive in both the literature and ethnographic interviews with conservation practitioners. It is tied to the idea that people from rural villages do not know how to manage their forests. I was constantly told that villagers needed to learn the skills to set up "successful land use management plans". Not only was it never made clear to me what these skills might be, it was also never indicated to me, by people from Maimafu, that they want to manage the land that they hold the rights to in any way other than the way that they do now. This is not to say that people do not want some sort of "police force" to keep others off of their land, they do. Men argue that violations of traditional tenure rules are not punished harshly enough these days. But no one indicated to me that they wanted to change their own behavior in any way.

According to the NGO people are a sustained threat to their environment. They are not seen as the producers of the environment. As I have shown elsewhere the cultural practices in Maimafu have added to the biological diversity in the area (West 2000:97). The absence of pigs in Maimafu, due to adherence to Seventh-day Adventist taboos against the consumption of pork, and thus the lack of pig disturbance in the surrounding forests, has added to the biological diversity. In addition, land discursively produced as "remote" and without "human disturbance" is land that has been used for hunting for many years. While on hunting trips men plant trees, alter landscapes, plant gardens, and conduct other environmental management techniques that produced the landscape that we see today.

The forests of Papua New Guinea are relatively unstudied compared to forests in other neo-tropical countries. They are highly biologically diverse and are seen as relatively intact by biological researchers (Sekhran and Miller 1994). Papua New Guinea has thus become the frontier for biological research and biological conservation. The biological diversity of Papua New Guinea is also discursively produced as having benefits (Beehler 1994:37). There appears to be an ethical mandate of sorts among biologists to protect this diversity and conservationists tend to speak of the worldwide implications for the loss of this diversity. The conservation biologists that I worked with see themselves as studying and protecting this biological diversity for the good of humanity. They see what they do as a moral imperative that perhaps transcends local rights. This seems to be the case with many conservationists and it is directly tied to their own personal experiences and the socio-cultural milieu of late modernity in the "west" (Taylor 2000).

This ethical mandate to conserve biodiversity is also reflected in the language of BCN. In one of their reports they state,

> Biodiversity represents the very foundation of human existence. Yet by our heedless actions we are eroding this biological capital at an alarming rate. Even today, despite the destruction that we have inflicted on the environment and its natural bounty, its resilience is taken for granted. But the more we learn of the workings of the natural world, the clearer it becomes that there is a limit to the disruption that the environment can endure.
>
> Beside the profound ethical and aesthetic implications, it is clear that the loss of biodiversity has serious economic and social costs. The genes, species, ecosystems and human knowledge which are being lost represent a living library of options available for adapting to local and global change. Biodiversity is part of our daily lives and livelihood and constitutes the resources upon which families, communities, nations and future generations depend. (BCN 1999:3)

Throughout this essay I have used the single category of "biologists" or "conservationists" to represent all of the people working with or for RCF or WCS. Here I wish to make a further distinction. Some of the biologists working for RCF are Papua New Guinean. These men, and they are all male, have a different sort of ethical justification for the importance of the conservation of biological diversity in Papua New Guinea than do expatriate conservation biologists from Australia and America. They do see all of the above reasons for conservation but they also, in a way very different from non-Papua New Guineans, see the biological diversity of their country as the one valuable resource that belongs to them. Due to World Bank/International Monetary Fund mandated structural adjustment programs, Papua New Guineans may not own the resource extraction companies (logging, mining, and oil) that work in their country. For Papua New Guinean biologists, biodiversity is seen as the only bargaining tool that their country has in the world market.

Conclusions

The people living within the boundaries of the Crater Mountain Wildlife Management Area are characterized by NGOs as both ignorant of and threatening to their environments. By using anthropologically based terminology to discuss indigenous or local peoples, NGOs give the illusion of attention being paid to local social practices and social relations that affect biological diversity. Yet, as I have shown in this chapter, in the case of the Crater Mountain project conservation biologists employ these terms without an understanding of their meaning, the extensive ethnographic literature concerning Gimi speakers, or the very basics of local cultural articulations. There is no acknowledgment on the part of the NGO that the current inhabitants of Maimafu village and their ancestors created, through their cultural relations with nature, the very environment which conservation biologists wish to protect.

It is ironic that there is such a full-scale failure to acknowledge the local production of nature given the recent growth of literature on "local knowledge" or "indigenous knowledge" in conservation and development circles. Sillitoe (1998a and 1998b), who has written extensively about local knowledge both theoretically and ethnographically in the PNG context, argues that

> Local knowledge in development contexts may relate to any knowledge held collectively by a population, informing interpretation of the world. It may encompass any domain in development, particularly that pertaining to natural resource management ... It is conditioned by socio-cultural tradition, being culturally relative understanding inculcated into individuals from birth, structuring how they interface with their environments. (1998a:204)

Elsewhere (Ellis and West 2004), Ellis and I have argued that accepted definitions of local or indigenous knowledge must be taken further with respect to local history, biology, and economics. Yet, even with this critique of the indigenous knowledge literature, I take seriously the anthropological fact that people know things about their environments. I do not argue that local people are somehow "ecologically noble savages" but rather that the current social practices of people in Maimafu, as they are both related to and separate from the environment, have emerged over time and have given local people unique ways in which to cognize their environment. I also argue that this unique cognition, which is historically contingent, should be taken into account by anyone who wishes to understand environmental change over time in the Crater Mountain area. The constant discursive production of Gimi speaking peoples as threats to their environment elides this local knowledge, silences local environmental history, and disregards what some would argue is the lifeblood of anthropology: the analysis of local social/environmental relations.

In the introduction to this essay I cited Brosius's argument that environmentally focused discourses "define various forms of agency, administer certain silences, and prescribe various forms of intervention" (Brosius 1999:277–278). Through the discursive analysis of the co-opting of anthropological terms by conservation biologists, the production of residents of Maimafu as indigenous people "fallen from grace", the use of the tropes of paternity and cargo, and the constant production of local people as threats to their natural environments I have demonstrated what Brosius argues. These discursive productions define agency, allow silences, and proscribe interventions. They create a conservation reality based on an imagined primitive and a misuse of anthropological ideas.

Conservationists either ignore the rich body of ethnographic data available about Gimi speakers or misinterpret and misrepresent this data. They co-opt anthropological terms as a shorthand and thus misrepresent the Gimi. This misuse pushes me as an anthropologist to do certain kinds of research in reaction/response such as the discursive analysis contained in this essay. The conservationists associated with the Crater Mountain project have noble intentions but their effectiveness in providing development options and in understanding the human uses of biological diversity are hampered by the lack of attention they pay to anthropological data.

In the past two decades anthropologists have examined the role of anthropology, and ethnography in particular, in the production of the other and in silencing "subaltern voices". This critique of ethnography and anthropological practice is serious business and has forced the discipline to examine the power relations implicit in our profession (Appadurai 1988; Clifford and Marcus 1986; Fabian 1983; Friedman 1990; Marcus and Fischer 1986).[13] One of the many responses to these criticisms is the disciplinary push for transnational multi-sited research focusing upon the connections between local sites and global processes (see Featherstone 1990; Gupta and Ferguson 1992; Marcus 1995). I consider my research to fall squarely within this newer form of anthropological practice.

I have been trained in entirety in a post-modern anthropology which espouses a critique of ethnographic authority. I began graduate school in 1991 and never had a relationship with the idea of writing ethnography that was not fraught with, yet made fascinating by, questions about authority, text production, power, and representation. I never thought that I would be attempting to understand or describe "a physically and symbolically enclosed world" (Marcus 1998:109). I also had no idea about the real complexities that would be involved in managing my relationships with participants in a research project where differences between participants' access to power were so profound.

Multi-sited ethnography moves the ethnographer between sites and groups of differently situated individuals. During one project an ethnographer might work with people from very different circumstances. This multiplicity of subject positions creates an at once more complex and less complex ethnographic situation. It is more complex in that working out relations with many different individuals forces you to be constantly aware of class, gender, age, education level, race, and ethnicity and to be mindful of how these factors are affecting your relations and your behavior. On the other hand it is less complex in that not all relations are embedded in morally loaded circumstances like colonialism (Marcus 1997:121).

The power relations in multi-sited ethnographic work are different from those in traditional ethnography. Dealing with multiply positioned subjects means that power relations become more ambiguous than in the past when anthropologists dealt with informants from one or two social or ethnic groups. In the past the anthropologist may have been assumed to be in the dominant position in terms of these relations; now that cannot always be assumed. The anthropologist moves from subordinate to dominant and back again depending upon the informant/participant she is working with at the time (Marcus 1998:121).

Within this new social milieu in which NGOs have the power to represent the traditional subjects of ethnographic inquiry we are faced with a question; in our anthropological practice do we eschew the traditional subjects and practices of anthropological research that have been so critically examined over the past twenty years in favor of a kind of anthropology that focuses on the multiplicity of transnational connections between multiply positioned actors and groups? Or do we take seriously the fact that NGOs have become the new early twentieth-century anthropology? By this I mean that NGOs now have the power to discursively produce "local peoples", "indigenous peoples", "peasants", and such and have their productions taken very seriously. Can we work within the critique of traditional anthropology to counter these discursive productions in a way that neither essentializes local people and their lives nor deconstructs them to the point of powerlessness?

In my work I write about the "unintended consequences" of conservation and development interventions in Papua New Guinea. One such consequence is that I have been forced to try to do precisely what I have questioned above. This essay is part of that attempt. It is part of a critical ethnographic practice that takes seriously the social relations of late modernity while at the same time counters the problematic discursive productions produced and acted upon by NGOs.

Acknowledgments

I would like to acknowledge funding from The Wenner-Gren Foundation for Anthropological Research (Gr. 6219) and The National Science Foundation (SBR-9707719). I would also like to thank Pamela J. Stewart, Andrew Strathern, J. Peter Brosius, Crystal L. Fortwangler, Dorothy Hodgson, George E. B. Morren, Bonnie J. McCay, J.C. Salyer, Neil Smith, Patricia H. West and the editors of Social Analysis for insightful comments on earlier drafts of this chapter.

Notes

1. Here and elsewhere (West 2000), I take "discourse" to mean any and all verbal and textual productions. This includes reports, stories, conversations, images, pictures, and all other kinds of linguistic and visual representations.
2. The history of integrated conservation and economic development projects and the history of the Crater Mountain project in particular is addressed extensively elsewhere (West 2000).
3. Elsewhere (West 2000:158), I discuss the "development" projects implemented in New Guinea by colonial governments and argue that contemporary development interventions which propose to link conservation and development mirror these historic colonial interventions.
4. Perhaps most importantly, the purveyors of these projects failed to discuss or analyze a concern that should have been central in their thought: there is a "tendency toward a reduction in species diversity in many commodity based systems" (Schroeder 1995:327; see Shiva 1992).
5. Maimafu is a settlement of 800 people located in the mountains of Papua New Guinea's Eastern Highlands Province. Residents of Maimafu practice shifting cultivation on their ancestral lands, and gardening is their main subsistence activity. People also collect "wild" foods from the forest, and coffee, the only significant cash crop, is tended year round, and is harvested from late July through October. Most individuals in Maimafu claim membership in the Seventh-day Adventist (SDA) Church. Residents of Maimafu speak Unavisa Gimi, a sub-dialect of the West Gimi dialect of the Gimi language (DeLoach and Troolin 1988:7). Maimafu is located at the border between what have become known within anthropology as the "central highlands" and the "highlands fringe" culture areas (Hyndman and Morren 1990; Hays 1993). The Gimi speaking peoples of the Eastern Highlands have been the subjects of a fairly extensive ethnographic literature.
   There is no road to Maimafu and the community currently maintains a small airstrip, which is serviced twice a week by SDA Aviation and once weekly by Mission Aviation Fellowship (MAF). Since the village has no trade stores, all outside products and goods must be ordered through SDA Aviation or else purchased by individuals elsewhere and then brought back to the village. Residents maintain both a government school and a village aide post, but during the period of my fieldwork, there was only one teacher at the school (a long-time resident), and there was no medicine in the aid post. Maimafu has one elected village councilor who holds a seat in the provincial government that meets in Goroka. In the past three years there have been three United States Peace Corps volunteer couples in the village.
6. The contradiction in BCN's rationale is as follows: the entire project, which tests the hypothesis that increased local participation in commodity based systems relying on biodiversity will lead to higher levels of biological diversity (that the commodification of natural resources will ultimately save them) is based upon the premise which states that nature or the environment is always already commodified in that it is "natural capital". The BCN solution to the problem of "the destruction that we have inflicted on the environment and its natural bounty" through global commodity production is the further integration of "out-of-the-way" places where there is much *in situ* biological diversity into commodity based systems. Commodification apparently serves as the solution to commodification.
7. I came to Papua New Guinea as an "independent" anthropologist, with my own funding and was not hired by the Gimi or the NGOs working at Crater Mountain.
8. Gimi speakers are the subjects of an extensive literature. For a more extensive treatment of social organization and kinship, see Gillison (1987, 1993:25–61) and Glick (1963, 1967); for an analysis of Gimi speakers conceptions of their natural environment, see Glick (1964) and Gillison (1980); for discussion of the connections between mythological beliefs and cultural practices, see Gillison (1991, 1993).

9. This was not the case with the Papua New Guinean biologists working with RCF. They, having lived in these rural villages as resident biologists, understood local systems. But, again and again during my fieldwork suggestions from Papua New Guinean staff members with regard to implementing this project in ways that took local sociality into account were dismissed.
10. Elsewhere I discuss the role of the media in the production of biologists' notions of indigenous people and notions of whiteness held by residents of Maimafu (West 2000:196).
11. Esta and Nara are pseudonyms for my assistants. Both of the assistants were nineteen years old and fluent in English, Melanesian Pidgin, and Unavisa Gimi.
12. "Namatai sa waname ya ahloha. Namatai sa waname su mehe gehe. Kau bai gehe. Namatai sa waname ohku ahloahtine namaya hoah". Translated by Esta and Nara, January 12, 1998.
13. Even with this critique, anthropology is still "predicated on the fact of otherness and difference, on the lively, informative thrust supplied to it by what is strange or foreign" (Said 1989:213).

References

Appadurai, A. 1988 "Introduction: Place and Voice in Anthropological Theory". *Cultural Anthropology* 3(1):16–20.

Beehler, Bruce M. 1993 "Biodiversity and Conservation of Warm-Blooded Vertebrates of Papua New Guinea". In B. Beehler (ed) *Papua New Guinea Conservation Needs Assessment Report, Volume 2*. A Biodiversity Analysis for Papua New Guinea. Washington, D.C.: Biodiversity Support Program.

BCN 1996 *Biodiversity Conservation Network 1996 Annual Report: Stories from the Field and Lessons Learned*. Biodiversity Support Program, Washington, D.C.

——— 1997 *Biodiversity Conservation Network 1997 Annual Report: Getting Down to Business*. Biodiversity Support Program, Washington, D.C.

——— 1998 *Biodiversity Conservation Network 1998 Annual Report: Getting Down to Business*. Biodiversity Support Program, Washington, D.C.

——— 2000 *In Good Company: Effective Alliances for Conservation*. Biodiversity Support Program, Washington, D.C.

Bonner, R. 1994 *At the Hand of Man: Peril and Hope for Africa's Wildlife*. New York: Vintage Press.

Brandon, K. and M. Wells 1992 "Planning for People and Parks: Design Dilemmas". *World Development* 20 (4):557–570.

Brown, M. and B. Wyckoff-Baird 1992 *Designing Integrated Conservation and Development Projects*. Washington, D.C.: The Biodiversity Support Program.

Blinkoff, R. n.d. "Caretaking and Companionship: Portraying Property Relations in Sokamin, Papua New Guinea". Paper presented for the Roskilde Training Seminar on Negotiating Property and Vindicating Land Claims. October 1999, Denmark.

Brosius, J.P. 1999 "Anthropological Engagements with Environmentalism". *Current Anthropology* 40 (3):277–309.

Clifford, J. and G.E. Marcus (eds) 1986 *Writing Culture: The Poetics and Politics of Ethnography*. Berkeley: University of California Press.

DeLoach, E. and D. Troolin 1988 *Contact Survey Report of the Gimi Language, Western Dialect*. Ukarumpa: Summer Institute of Linguistics.

Ellis D.M. and P. West 2004 "Local History as 'Indigenous Knowledge': Aeroplanes, in Haia and Maimafu, Papua New Guinea". In A. Bicker, P. Sillitoe, and J. Pottier (eds) *Investigating Local Knowledge: New Directions, New Approaches*. London: Ashgate.

Fabian, J. 1983 *Time and the Other: How Anthropology Makes Its Objects*. New York: Columbia University Press.

Featherstone, M. (ed) 1990 *Global Culture: Nationalism, Globalization and Modernity*. London: Sage Publications.

Feinberg, R. 1995 "Introduction: Politics of Culture in the Pacific Islands". *Ethnology* 34(2):91–98.

Friedman, J. 1990 "Being in the World: Globalization and Localization". In M. Featherstone (ed) *Global Culture: Nationalism, Globalization and Modernity*. London: Sage Publications.

Gillison, G. 1980 "Images of Nature in Gimi Thought". In C. MacCormack and M. Strathern (eds) *Nature, Culture and Gender*. Cambridge: Cambridge University Press.

——— 1987 "Incest and the Atom of Kinship: The Role of the Mother's Brother in a New Guinea Highlands Society". *Ethos* 15:166–202.

——— 1991 "The Flute Myth and the Law of Equivalence: Origins of a Principle of Exchange". In M. Godelier and M. Strathern (eds) *Big and Great Men: Personifications of Power in Melanesia*. Cambridge: Cambridge University Press.

——— 1993 *Between Culture and Fantasy: A New Guinea Highlands Mythology*. Chicago and London: The University of Chicago Press.

Glick, L.B. 1963 "Foundations of a Primitive Medical System: The Gimi of the New Guinea Highlands". Ph.D. diss., Graduate School of Arts and Sciences, University of Pennsylvania.

——— 1964 "Categories and Relations in Gimi Natural Science". *American Anthropologist* 66 (2):273–280.

——— 1967 "The Role of Choice in Gimi Kinship". *Southwestern Journal of Anthropology* 23:371–382.

Gupta, A. and J. Ferguson 1992 "Beyond 'Culture': Space, Identity, and the Politics of Difference". *Cultural Anthropology* 7(1):6–23.

Hays, T.E. 1993 "The New Guinea Highlands: Region, Culture Area, or Fuzzy Set?" *Current Anthropology* 34(2):141–163.

Hecht, S. and A. Cockburn 1990 *The Fate of the Forest: Developers, Destroyers, and Defenders of the Amazon*. New York: HarperCollins.

Hobsbawm, E. and T. Ranger (eds) 1983 *The Invention of Tradition*. Cambridge: Cambridge University Press.

Hyndman, D. and G.E.B. Morren Jr. 1990 "The Human Ecology of the Mountain-Ok of Central New Guinea: A Regional and Inter-regional Approach". In B. Craig and D. Hyndman (eds) *Children of Afek: Tradition and Change among the Mountain-Ok of Central New Guinea*. Oceania Monograph 40: University of Sydney.

Johnson, A. 1997 "Processes for Effecting Community Participation in the Establishment of Protected Areas: A Case Study of the Crater Mountain Wildlife Management Area". In C. Filer (ed) *The Political Economy of Forest Management in Papua New Guinea*. Boroko: National Research Institute (Monograph 32), Papua New Guinea; London: International Institute for Environment and Development.

Jolly, M. and N. Thomas (eds) 1992 *The Politics of Tradition in the Pacific*. Oceania 62(4). Special edition.

Kahn, M. 2000 "Tahiti Intertwined: Ancestral Land, Tourist Postcard, and Nuclear Test Site". *American Anthropologist* 102(1):7–26.

Kaplan, M. 1995 *Neither Cargo nor Cult: Ritual Politics and the Colonial Imagination in Fiji*. Durham: Duke University Press.

Keesing, R. and R. Tonkinson (eds) 1982 *Reinventing Traditional Culture: The Politics of Kastom in Island Melanesia*. Mankind 13(4). Special issue.

Lindstrom, L. and G.M. White 1990 *Island Encounters*. Washington, D.C.: Smithsonian Institution Press.

Linnekin, J. 1992 "On the Theory and Politics of Cultural Construction in the Pacific". *Oceania* 62(4):249–270.

Marcus, G. 1995 "Ethnography in/of the World System: The Emergence of Multi-sited Ethnography". *Annual Review of Anthropology* 24:95–117.

——— 1997 "The Uses of Complicity in the Changing Mise-en-Scene of Anthropological Fieldwork". *Representations* 59 (Summer 1997):95–117.

——— 1998 "Ethnography in/of the World System: The Emergence of Multi-sited Ethnography". In G. Marcus, *Ethnography Through Thick and Thin*. Princeton: Princeton University Press.

Marcus, G. E. and M. J. Fischer 1986 *Anthropology as Cultural Critique: An Experimental Moment in the Human Sciences*. Chicago: University of Chicago Press.

Morren, G.E.B. Jr. 1986 *The Miyanmin: Human Ecology of a Papua New Guinea Society*. UMI Studies in Cultural Anthropology, no. 9. Ann Arbor: University of Michigan Press.

Pearl, M. C. 1994 "Local Initiatives and the Rewards for Biodiversity Conservation: Crater Mountain Wildlife Management Area, Papua New Guinea". In D. Western, R.M. Wright, and S.C. Strum (eds) *Natural Connections: Perspectives in Community-Based Conservation*, Washington, D.C.: Island Press.

Pred, A. and M.J. Watts 1992 *Reworking Modernity: Capitalism and Symbolic Discontent*. New Brunswick: Rutgers University Press.

RCF and WCS 1995 "Crater Mountain Wildlife Management Area: A Model for Testing the Linkage of Community-Based Enterprises with Conservation of Biodiversity" (BCN Implementation Grant Proposal, RCF & WCS)

Sachs, W. 1993 "Global Ecology in the Shadow of 'Development'". In W. Sachs (ed) *Global Ecology*. London: Zed Books.

Said, E.W. 1989 "Representing the Colonized: Anthropology's Interlocutors". *Critical Inquiry* 15:205–225.

Sekhran, N. and S. Miller 1994 "Introduction and Summary". In N. Sekhran and S. Miller (eds) *Papua New Guinea Country Study on Biological Diversity*. A report to the United Nations Environment Program, Waigani, Papua New Guinea, Department of Environment and Conservation, Conservation Resource Centre; and Nairobi, Kenya, African Centre for Resources and Environment (ACRE).

Schroeder, R. 1993 "Shady Practice". *Economic Geography* 69(4):349–365.

——— 1995 "Contradictions along the Commodity Road to Environmental Stabilization". *Antipode* 27(4).

Shiva, V. 1992 *The Future of Progress: Reflections on Environment and Development*. Bristol: International Society for Ecology and Culture.

Sillitoe, P. 1998a "What, Know Natives? Local Knowledge in Development". *Social Anthropology* 6 (2):203–220.

——— 1998b "The Development of Indigenous Knowledge: A New Applied Anthropology". *Current Anthropology* 39(2).

Taussig, M. 1987 *Shamanism, Colonialism and the Wild Man*. Chicago: University of Chicago Press.

Taylor, D. 2000 "The Rise of the Environmental Justice Paradigm". *American Behavioral Scientist* 43(4):508–580.

Tsing, A.L. 1993 *In the Realm of the Diamond Queen: Marginality in an Out-of-the-Way Place*. Princeton: Princeton University Press.

Wapner, P. 1996 *Environmental Activism and World Civic Politics*. Albany: State University of New York Press.

Weeks, P. 1999 "Cyber-activism: World Wildlife Fund's Campaign to Save the Tiger". *Culture and Agriculture* 21(3):19–30.

Wells, M. and K. Brandon 1992 *People and Parks: Linking Protected Area Management with Local Communities*. Washington, D.C.: The World Bank.

West, P. 2000 "The Practices, Ideologies, and Consequences of Conservation and Development in Papua New Guinea." Doctoral dissertation submitted in partial fulfillment for the Ph.D. in Anthropology, February 18, 2000. Rutgers University: New Brunswick, N.J.

White, G.M. and L. Lindstrom (eds) 1993 *Custom Today in Oceania. Anthropological Forum 6*. Special Edition.

Whitehouse, H. 1995 *Inside the Cult: Religious Innovation and Transmission in Papua New Guinea.* Oxford: Oxford University Press.

Wildlife Conservation Society 1995 *The Crater Mountain Wildlife Management Area Recommendations for Developing a Natural Resources Management Plan.* Bronx: The Wildlife Conservation Society.

Wolf, E.R. 1982 *Europe and the People Without History.* Berkeley: University of California Press.

Worsley, P. 1968 *The Trumpet Shall Sound: A Study of "Cargo" Cults in Melanesia.* New York: Stockton.

Chapter 4

THE POLITICS OF ACCOUNTABILITY
An Institutional Analysis of the Conservation
Movement in Papua New Guinea

John Richard Wagner

Introduction

The conservation movement in Papua New Guinea today is dominated by global interests and global agencies. This has especially been the case since the Rio Summit of 1992 and the signing of the UN Convention on Biological Diversity. Shortly after the Summit, the United Nations Environment Programme commissioned the first comprehensive study of biodiversity in Papua New Guinea (PNG), reporting that the country "harbors more than five percent of the world's biodiversity in less than one percent of its land area" (Sekhran and Miller 1994:6). In response to these findings, The PNG Biodiversity Conservation and Resource Management Programme was set up in 1993, with funding provided by the Global Environment Facility. The administrators of this program moved quickly, in the first year of their operation, to set up an integrated conservation and development project in Lak, New Ireland, and in 1995 a second project was set up in the Bismarck-Ramu area. The biodiversity program also provides logistical support for several other projects scattered throughout the country, which are being facilitated by a variety of national and international NGOs.[1]

The integrated conservation and development approach has emerged over the past two decades as a global response to the problems created by a previous generation of conservation projects. The main problem with the projects of the 1960s and 1970s was that they had ignored the rights and needs of local communities, forcibly excluding them from areas they had long relied on for key resources (Brown and Wyckoff 1992; McCallum and Sekhran 1997; Wells 1992). Predictably, such communities resisted their forcible displacement from traditional use areas, and continued to use protected areas *illegally*, thus undermining conservation efforts. In order to avoid this problem, many conservation groups now attempt to work in partnership with local communities, and are attempting to integrate conservation and development goals when they plan their projects. Quite appropriately, this has become the dominant approach in PNG where almost the entire land surface of the country is owned by local communities and kin groups, rather than by government or private individuals or corporations. Thus, today's conservation movement in PNG, while driven and funded by global interests, must also answer to the needs and aspirations of rural communities.

Unfortunately the integrated approach to conservation and development has not produced many success stories in PNG or elsewhere. Critics argue that the approach moves too slowly, and does not allow conservation regimes to be put in place quickly enough to halt the rapid loss of biodiversity that is occurring worldwide.[2] Despite the sense of urgency that necessarily surrounds efforts to achieve successful outcomes, I believe it is premature at this point to make sweeping generalizations about success or failure in PNG, where this approach is less than a decade old and many projects are still in their infancy. In their initial stages these projects require that an extremely divergent group of organizations learn to communicate effectively with one another, set common goals, and create effective institutions for the implementation of project activities. What is needed now is a constructive program of monitoring and assessment that can be used to inform project planning and implementation, and enhance the likelihood of positive outcomes (Margoluis and Salafsky 1998; Wells 1992).

In this chapter I will be addressing one particularly troublesome issue that I believe has received far too little attention to date—the issue of accountability. Since conservation and development projects are implemented by transnational coalitions of grassroots organizations, national and international NGOs and government agencies, no single organization is accountable for the overall outcomes of a given project. Accountability in this context is *relational*.[3] It depends on the ability of project partners to create an institutional framework within which they can communicate effectively and clearly define and carry out their respective roles and responsibilities. In the absence of such a framework, each organization, by default, will tend to make decisions in accordance with the narrower set of goals that defines its own ideology and self-interest. Conflict rather than cooperation then becomes the rule, and no effective system of accountability can be created.

Funding insecurity appears to be one of the main causes of poor accountability in conservation projects throughout PNG and elsewhere. Under current arrangements, conservation and development projects are generally implemented by national NGOs that receive funding from one or more international donor organizations. Since this funding is usually provided on a short-term basis, the national NGOs are involved in a constant struggle to secure new funds and new donors, and in effect must *compete* for those funds against similar organizations. They thus come under pressure to misrepresent project outcomes in certain circumstances, in order to preserve their own institutional stability and keep their projects afloat. When it comes to research, they are also under pressure to spend their limited funds on the gathering of information that will improve their success in the funding competition, as opposed to the information actually needed for successful project implementation. Social science research, in this context, becomes an under-utilized resource since it is less amenable to promotional uses than is research that documents the unique ecological characteristics of a given conservation area.

In the analysis that follows, I will rely mainly on research I carried out in 1998–1999 in the village of Lababia—the site of the Kamiali[4] Integrated Conservation and Development Project. I went to Lababia to carry out doctoral research, seeking to document the resource use patterns of the community, and the ways in which those patterns were changing in response to the Kamiali Project and development pressures in general. Through my previous contacts with individuals involved in the project, I was aware that it had been implemented without the benefit of detailed information about the community's land tenure system, their social structure, political institutions, or economy. In support of the broad goals of the project, I therefore designed my research along the lines of a voluntary consultancy,[5] setting out to gather the type of information I felt would be necessary for the effective planning and implementation of such a project.

The Kamiali Integrated Conservation and Development Project

The Kamiali Project is located in a coastal region of Morobe Province, approximately 80 km south of Lae, the provincial capital. Lababia, the only community involved in the project, is home to 500 people who make their living through swidden agriculture and fishing. Lababia territory makes an excellent choice as a conservation area. It possesses a number of unusual ecological characteristics, and unusually high biodiversity values have been reported for both marine and terrestrial environments (Bein 1998).

The Kamiali Project is being managed by Village Development Trust (VDT), a national NGO based in Lae. Since its inception in 1989, VDT has grown into one of the largest NGOs in the country, and has been especially active as an advocate of sustainable forestry practices. They have obtained funding for the Kamiali Project from a wide range of overseas donors, including the World Wide Fund for Nature (WWF), the Dutch Interchurch Organization for Development Cooperation (ICCO), AusAid (an Australian government aid agency), the World Bank, the Swedish

Society for Nature Conservation, and the High Commissions of Australia, Canada and New Zealand.

During my period of research, VDT were employing two full-time staff members to manage the Kamiali Project—a project director and a field assistant. Most important decisions, however, were made jointly by VDT's senior management staff, a group of three to four people that included the project director. This group consulted regularly with an eight to ten person village committee known as the Kamiali Conservation Project Committee (KCPC). This committee was created in the initial stages of the project to serve as a liaison group between VDT and the village, and to assist in planning and implementing project activities. Donor organizations do not participate directly in the project. Most simply send field officers for an annual round of meetings with VDT staff in Lae, followed by a short visit to the village where they will be introduced to the village committee and other community representatives.

The Kamiali Project grew out of an earlier, unsuccessful conservation initiative known as the Lasanga Island/Lake Trist Project. VDT had implemented this project in 1992 with the intention of establishing a 250,000 hectare conservation area that would have extended 40 km along the Morobe coastline, from Lababia in the north to Siboma in the south. VDT had targeted this area for conservation because it was a relatively pristine area that was then under threat from industrial logging. A company based in the Philippines, Timber Producers and Marketing Corporation, had begun operating in the area in 1990. The conservation project collapsed in 1994, once it became obvious that village sentiment overall was not opposed to industrial logging. Of the four communities involved in the conservation project, only Lababia refused to allow logging in their territory.

After the collapse of the Lasanga Island Project, VDT continued their work with Lababia and in 1995 the two parties agreed to implement the much smaller Kamiali Project. The village agreed to the establishment of a conservation area that includes almost the whole of their claimed territory—an area of 43,400 hectares.[6] On September 1, 1996, this area was gazetted as a Wildlife Management Area under the authority of the country's Fauna Protection and Control Act. Rules were created so as to allow villagers to continue their traditional activities within this area, but to prohibit industrial activities and the use of introduced technologies, such as firearms for hunting, that were considered inappropriate for a conservation area. For their part, VDT agreed to finance construction of a village-wide water supply system, and to sponsor a number of economic development initiatives. These included a village fishing cooperative, a women's drum oven bakery, a micro-enterprise loans program, an eco-forestry project, and the construction in the village of a training center/guesthouse facility. VDT planned to use the center to run eco-forestry training programs, and when not in use for that purpose, to rent out rooms to tourists and to scientists wishing to conduct studies in the Wildlife Management Area.

By the time I arrived in Lababia in September 1998, the water supply was nearing completion and the training center/guesthouse had been constructed and was in operation. The center was not generating much revenue, however, and all the other economic development initiatives had collapsed. Over the next few months villagers became increasingly frustrated with VDT's lack of ability to deliver on its many "promises", and disillusioned by their slowness in responding to village complaints. By the end of January 1998, tempers had reached the breaking point, and villagers decided to shut down the project until all outstanding issues were resolved.

A review of the project's economic development initiatives makes it clear that planning activities were not informed by an adequate body of socio-economic information. The village committee, KCPC, had little or no experience in running small businesses, and had to rely on VDT to collect whatever information was necessary to the planning process. VDT has consistently underestimated the value of such information, however, and for strategic reasons, has preferred to spend their research dollars in other areas. Socio-economic information does not have the same *political* value as biological and ecological information.

Information Gathering as Political Strategy

Who is responsible for gathering together the kind of information necessary for the planning and effective implementation of a conservation and development project? The Biodiversity Support Program has published a guidebook for practitioners, in which a strong emphasis is placed on the need to gather a wide range of information prior to project implementation and throughout the duration of the project (Margoluis and Salafsky 1998). Unfortunately, the authors do not consider the issue of what institutional arrangements might best facilitate this process. Under current arrangements, donor organizations release funds to organizations like VDT without detailed knowledge of the information base being used to plan the project, and without contractual requirements that such research be done. Facilitating NGOs are thus on their own in setting research priorities, and often don't have the staff to carry out a comprehensive research program.

VDT *has* been able to obtain funds for biodiversity studies, and in 1997 and 1998 an extensive study was carried out of both land and marine portions of the Kamiali Wildlife Management Area. The study's executive summary makes the claim that "nowhere else on the Huon Gulf (or possibly PNG) can there be found a place where a pristine forest reaches right to the sea". Regarding the biodiversity of the area, the report states that "within a six kilometer transect one can observe mangrove and sago swamps, lowland tropical rainforest, hill forest, mountain forest and cloud-moss forest", and that "the coral reefs of Kamiali are among the most ecologically diverse and biologically productive in the world" (Bein 1998). This type of research is essential to the conservationist goals of the project, but it also has *strategic* value in relationship to fund-raising activities. It can be used to *promote* the project to donor organizations. Social science research does not offer the same strategic benefits to the project under the existing institutional regime. It is less amenable to promotional uses since it is as likely to highlight problems in the project as it is to document strengths, and it does not generate easy-to-apply planning formulas. In fact, it tends to make planning a more complex and demanding process.

With hindsight it is easy to identify a number of problems at Lababia that could have been avoided if the effort had been made to gather certain bodies of information before the implementation of programs. This is certainly true of the village fishing project that failed after just a few months of operation. VDT staff had done some research in this case. They had reviewed the information available from Momase Fisheries, a government agency that buys and sells fish and provides outreach services to local fishermen. This information included a baseline study of Lababia's artisanal fishery that had been carried out in 1992. VDT followed the preferences of the community in designing the project, which involved the purchase of a gasoline-powered dinghy, an icebox, and some fishing gear. It was agreed that the project would be run as a village-wide cooperative. A VDT staff member produced a cost analysis of the project, which indicated that the village was capable of capturing the weekly volume of fish necessary to make the project profitable (Martin 1998:116).

Unfortunately, three crucial pieces of information were missing from this analysis. Firstly, fish stocks at Lababia were in decline by the time the project was implemented in 1996. This became evident during the course of my own research, when I carried out a number of fishing trials with village fishermen, gathered up-to-date economic data regarding the volume of fish captured and sold in Lae, interviewed fisheries experts, and collected anecdotal information from villagers concerning their fishing activities since the 1960s.

The second type of information has to do with the social composition of fishing groups in this part of Morobe Province. Fishing groups are organized as kin groups that fish together and augment their catch when possible by buying fish from other villagers. Fish is bought in the village for about half the price it will sell for in Lae. These groups are not always concerned about whether they can make a profit at fishing, since they can subsidize their operation by transporting passengers and cargo as well as fish. Thus, the several fishing groups already operating in Lababia when the project was set up, had little motivation for joining the cooperative. In the face of declining fish stocks and competition from smaller fishing groups, the village project did not prove to be cost-effective.[7]

The third type of information has to do with transportation issues in general. There are no roads in and out of Lababia, so transportation is entirely by water. In the 1980s villagers had owned a diesel-powered boat which they operated on a cooperative basis. It was used for fishing in local waters, and for transporting fish, cargo and passengers to Lae. For a period of several years management responsibilities were rotated amongst a number of village men, with good results, but eventually someone mismanaged the operation, and the boat fell into disrepair. Villagers had this earlier experience in mind when they planned the 1996 fishing project, and in fact they chose the name of the former boat, *Mbame*, as the name of the new fishing group. During the 1990s, however, villagers had become accustomed to the use of gasoline-powered dinghies, which, while much more expensive to operate, are much faster. Politicians, it turns out, are responsible for the proliferation of these boats along the Morobe coast—as pay-offs to their political supporters. A number of village men told me they had argued in favor of a diesel-powered boat for the new project, but that the majority of men, younger men especially, insisted on a faster boat.

If sufficient time had been devoted to the gathering of all relevant information, many if not all of the problems associated with the fishing project, and the other small business ventures, could have been avoided. VDT did not have the resources, however, to carry out an extensive program of research, and villagers were impatient for action. Donor organizations, since they are in a "race for the rainforest" (McCallum and Sekhran 1997), feel pressured to disburse funds and implement projects before adequate knowledge is accumulated and shared amongst stakeholders. The need here is not just for better logistical planning around the gathering of information. The institutional design of these projects needs to be modified so as to create a system of accountability that takes information-gathering into account.

The Politics of Accountability

The frustrations that led villagers to shut down the Kamiali Project were not caused simply by the failure of the village fishing project and other small business ventures. Villagers were also frustrated by the fact that VDT seemed to be putting their own self-interest ahead of the interests of Lababia. In their conversations with me, villagers regularly emphasized the fact that VDT had grown enormously as an organization since the inception of the Kamiali Project, whereas life in the village had hardly changed at all. In 1992 VDT had only two or three staff members, a tiny rented office, and a single dilapidated vehicle. By September 1998 when I arrived, they had a full-time staff of about a dozen, several vehicles, and had purchased their own office and apartment compound in Lae. Rather than appreciating the newfound strength and professionalism of their urban partners, villagers began to suspect that VDT was appropriating funds intended for them.

Villagers were particularly incensed that VDT had bought a small pleasure craft for transporting guests back and forth to the training center. The money for the boat came from the New Zealand High Commission and was given in support of VDT's various educational programs. VDT intended to use the boat to run passengers to the Kamiali Training Center but also to other destinations along the coast. Villagers were upset because several months earlier they had also requested assistance from the High Commission to purchase a boat. They now suspected VDT of "stealing" what was rightfully theirs. The village's request had been a legitimate one since, as already mentioned, they had previously owned and operated their own diesel-powered boat, transporting passengers and commercial goods, such as fish, to markets in Lae. They wished to own and operate such a boat again, and to use it for the expanded operations that would now be possible as a result of training center activities. Since the VDT boat was clearly not appropriate for their needs, they began to feel that their own aspirations within the project were taking a backseat to those of VDT.

Villagers had a chance to question the High Commission staff member who had approved VDT's boat application, when he visited the Kamiali Training Center on July 25, 1999. He side-stepped their questions, however, indicating that it was a problem for VDT and the village to sort out. In conversation with me he emphasized that his mandate was simply to disburse funds for educational purposes to qualifying organizations, and that VDT was one of the most highly qualified organizations in the country (Shaw 1999). He did not have a mandate to fund village level economic development projects.

The boat incident illustrates the way in which project partners can end up working at cross-purposes with one another, when existing institutional arrangements do not accommodate any overall system of accountability. One of the main problems with current institutional arrangements lies in the fact that most donor organizations are not interested in playing a direct role in project activities. As a result they have a very limited understanding of grassroots issues, and no realistic way of assessing the overall impacts of their funding programs. The High Commission officer who approved VDT's boat application had no way of knowing that VDT and the community were already embroiled in a dispute over the issue. He expected that VDT would use the boat to transport workshop participants to and from the Kamiali Center, but in the end villagers banned the boat entirely from the village. None of the overseas donors that fund individual components of the Kamiali Project are accountable to villagers for project outcomes. Their accountability is to their own donors—governments, private individuals and corporations—and is satisfied by the filing of paper reports in overseas offices.

Accountability works differently at each level of the project hierarchy. VDT, as the organization that is actually implementing the project, is accountable to their donors *financially*, that is, they must be able to satisfy the donor that all funds were used for the purposes specified in their funding application. Donors are not in a position to hold VDT accountable for project outcomes however, or to evaluate the soundness of their planning activities. VDT also has important responsibilities toward their permanent staff—not a trivial consideration in a country where decent-paying, skilled jobs are in short supply. Finally VDT is accountable to the community of Lababia—but on what basis? During my stay in Lababia, villagers were not at all sure what to expect from VDT. On the most general level they expected "development", but VDT's responsibilities as a development agency have never been clearly defined.

At the village level accountability works in yet another way. KCPC, the village committee in charge of project activities, occupies an extremely difficult position in relation to their own community and to VDT. It was their responsibility to sit down with VDT staff to plan project activities, and then to bring those plans to the village for approval. Committee members had to seek approval for their decisions from a council of *bigmen*,[8] and, in some cases, from the village as a whole during a general meeting. During times when little progress was being made, or when contentious issues were being discussed, committee members regularly came in for bitter censure. Villagers viewed them as having a vested interest in the project, since they had access to the KCPC expense budget, and were paid modest per diems to compensate them for the time lost from other pursuits. VDT took responsibility for monitoring the committee's use of its budget, since it was them that provided the money. While committee members regularly complained about the small size of their budget, VDT staff complained that they mismanaged it, and refused to increase it until the committee became more *accountable*.

It is by no means an easy process to create the type of institutional framework within which these various systems of accountability can be integrated. Brown and Fox (1998:455) argue that accountability within transnational coalitions requires, as a precondition, that participating organizations achieve a certain degree of "social trust", and that this trust can only be achieved through "cycles of negotiation that bridge the gaps among their members—negotiations that deal with inevitable conflicts without destroying trust among the parties". The villagers' shutdown of the project did eventually lead to a new series of negotiations in which VDT staff and the village agreed to create a "partnership agreement". This was to be a contractual agreement signed by each party, that would clearly define their respective roles and responsibilities within the project.

The Partnership Agreement

Villagers were enthusiastic about the concept of a new "partnership agreement" and quickly appointed a committee of thirty people to carry forward the agreement process. The committee included one or more representatives from each clan in the village, as well as two women's representatives and all current KCPC members. The committee spent many hours reviewing the history of the project, debating key issues, and creating a draft agreement for presentation to VDT. Responsibility for writing the draft agreement was given to a villager who had long held a senior administrative position in the National Health Services Program of the Lutheran Church. This man had, in fact, resigned from his position with the Lutheran Church in order to return to Lababia and participate in the agreement process.

VDT staff, as it turned out, were far less committed than the villagers to creating a contractual partnership agreement. A meeting had been set up for March 10, 1999, at which village representatives were to provide VDT with a copy of their draft agreement, but a couple of days before this meeting, villagers were advised that there had been a "misunderstanding". VDT had not wanted the village to create a draft agreement. They simply wanted to hear villagers thoughts on the matter, and would then proceed to hold a series of meetings and workshops during which VDT staff and village representatives would jointly write up an agreement. The villagers I spoke to were convinced that there had not been any misunderstanding, and they once again became suspicious of VDT's motives.

At the March 10 meeting, villagers initially withheld their copy of the draft agreement, and sought instead to have VDT staff clarify their own position. It soon became apparent that VDT had no agreed-on position regarding either the content or the structure of the proposed partnership agreement. They gave no indication that they were even interested in creating the type of contractual agreement that the villagers were seeking. The meeting ended with vague reassurances from VDT that they were there to assist villagers, not boss them around, and that they would conscientiously read the draft agreement and respond to it in a couple of weeks. The villagers agreed to this and a further meeting was set up for that purpose.

Why are organizations like VDT reluctant to enter into contractual agreements with their village partners? Villagers at Lababia have *contracted* to set aside 43,400 hectares of their territory as a Wildlife Management Area, but receive no contractual assurances regarding the development components of the project. One obvious explanation is that environmental NGOs simply don't have the expertise to be developers, sustainable or otherwise—a problem that is not unique to the Kamiali Project.[9] In other cases, however, the cause appears to be ideological. In describing the Bismarck-Ramu Project administered by the PNG Biodiversity Programme, one researcher has written that, "there was a conscious attempt [at Bismarck-Ramu] to get away from the idea that there was a 'conservation for development' *transaction* built into the design of the project" (van Helden 2001:20).

Similarly, in the case of the Kamiali Project, VDT staff were not willing to enter into a contractual agreement with Lababia that would have formally acknowledged the transactional nature of their relationship. When VDT eventually responded to the villagers' draft, they did not make concrete proposals for what a final agreement might look like. Instead they proposed that the village create an entirely new type of community institution, referred to as a "community-based organization", or "CBO". This organization would be empowered to run and administer village-based businesses, to deal directly with donor organizations and government agencies, and to engage in community-planning activities within and beyond the scope of the Kamiali Project. This was not an entirely new proposal—VDT had previously run workshops at the Kamiali Training Center to inform villagers of this particular approach to community planning. The villagers had also made reference to the idea in their draft agreement. VDT now seized on the concept as a way of meeting the village's demands for greater control over project activities.

Village representatives responded enthusiastically to the CBO initiative, and in a show of good faith agreed to end their shutdown of the project. An intensive series of workshops and negotiations now began, in which VDT staff proposed that the CBO should be organized along the same lines as their own organization. They proposed writing up a constitution, setting up a Board of Directors, and registering the organization as a non-profit society under the country's Associations Act. The Board of Directors was to be composed of four village representatives, two VDT staff members, and a private businessman from Lae. It was also intended that the new organization would replace KCPC, and would have a large enough budget to hire a permanent staff, including an Executive Director. VDT staff stated that there were several overseas donor organizations that preferred to fund community based organizations directly, rather than channel funds through urban-based NGOs.

Having set out to resolve their conflicts through the negotiation of a contractual partnership agreement, the two parties now found themselves involved in an ambitious program of institutional innovation. Unfortunately, there are no clear precedents, or models, to guide this type of planning process. I believe it is possible, however, to borrow a model from common property theory, and use it to predict the kind of direction in which this type of institutional innovation should proceed.

The Institutional Design of Common Property Systems

In my own research at Lababia, I took as my starting point the fact that the community and their territory constitute a type of common property resource system. The community as a whole lays claim to the area defined as the Kamiali Wildlife Management Area, on the basis of historic use and occupation, and on the basis of national legislation that recognizes the authority of customary landowning groups. Various kin groups lay claim to specific portions of that territory, also based on historic usage, while strong individual rights are exercised over certain types of land—garden areas cleared from primary forest, for example. Patterns of resource use within this territory are organized and defined by a distinct set of practices and rules that, for the most part, are under the control of the community. The national government plays virtually no role in the management of resources within Lababia's territory.

Resource use practices at Lababia, over a period of several centuries at least, have had minimal impact on the physical environment. Commercial fish stocks are in decline but those species represent a very small portion of the many species present in the area. The land areas used for agriculture represent only about 5 percent of the total land area within Lababia territory. The sustainability of this system, however, is now perceived to be at risk. The project was implemented as a response to the risk posed to the system by the activities of industrial logging companies. In more general terms the system is at risk due to an intensification of resource use due to rising population, and an increasing demand for cash. Villagers are thus faced with the challenge of having to change the rules by which they manage their common property resources, without undermining the long-term sustainability of those resources.

From this perspective, the primary goal of the Kamiali Project should be to support and enhance villagers' capacity to manage their resources in a sustainable way within the mixed economy that now characterizes this region. Since the project itself should be viewed as only a temporary intervention in a common property system, its institutional design should correspond to that which researchers have found to be characteristic of successful common property systems (see Ostrom 1990, 1992; Pinkerton and Weinstein 1995; Wade 1988). One of the most fundamental characteristics of successful systems is their *autonomous* nature—that is, management decisions are made by the local community, not by outsiders. This tends not to be the case in conservation and development projects, where decision-making activities are scattered amongst the various partners of a transnational coalition. Common property theory suggests that the institutions created to manage such projects should be more fully grounded in the institutional and customary practices of local communities.

It is also the case, however, as Elinor Ostrom (1990:101) has emphasized, that common property systems operate as part of larger systems, and that management rules and governance activities are often organized in "multiple layers of nested enterprises". Ostrom illustrates this point through discussion of irrigation systems in Spain and the Philippines, where local and regional associations form an integrated management system. She also emphasizes the fact that such associations are integrated into "local, regional, and national governmental jurisdictions", and that the rules that exist at each level must be congruent (Ostrom 1990:102). In the case of Lababia, governmental jurisdictions have limited scope although they do serve to legitimize villagers' landownership rights, and their control over local resources. It is in fact the conservation and development NGOs that play the more prominent role. In response to the poor performance of the national government in PNG, NGOs are becoming a kind of government by default, providing basic development services to many rural communities throughout the country. It is thus the NGO movement that provides the institutional infrastructure within which Lababia must integrate its own management system.

To what extent is the CBO approach at Lababia consistent with the common property approach described here? As villagers and VDT staff set about designing the CBO, it seemed glaringly obvious to me that the proposed organization bore no relationship to existing institutional practices at Lababia. By contrast, KCPC had been similar in structure to many other village committees, such as those that looked after the church and the community school. KCPC also appeared to be fairly well integrated into the overall political structure of the community. They acted under the authority of the council of village *bigmen*, the most important political institution in the village, and were either appointed or elected by the community as a whole. The CBO, however, was being created without any reference to existing customs in the village. When I questioned VDT's Executive Director about this, he suggested that the new organization should not be answerable to village *bigmen*. In reference to his own home community in West New Britain Province, he argued that *bigmen* take too long to make decisions, and often do not have the education required to understand the issues at hand. He proposed that the staff of the new organization should *consult* with village *bigmen*, and with the village as a whole, but that the CBO should be the final authority on development issues and management of the conservation area.

Given time, it is possible that the CBO will be integrated into the village's existing political institutions, despite the rather extreme position taken by VDT's Executive Director. When I discussed this issue with villagers, many seemed ill at ease with the notion that the CBO might challenge the authority of village *bigmen*. The individual who had recently resigned his administrative position with the Lutheran Church in order to return to the village, was emphatic in repudiating the position taken by VDT's Executive Director, insisting that they would look after that issue in their own way, without interference from VDT, and without any radical departure from existing practices. This man was himself very enthusiastic about the CBO concept, and it was clear that he would play a major role in the new organization.

The CBO approach also creates the possibility for the community to regain some of the authority it lost in earlier stages of the project, and to establish its own direct relationship with donor organizations. This could result in better communication amongst project partners and a more community-based approach to management, but there is no reason to assume that these possibilities will be realized. The CBO approach does not directly address any of the underlying problems of accountability discussed in this essay, and thus risks repeating the mistakes of the past. The problems associated with funding insecurity could in fact be exacerbated once money begins to flow directly to the CBO from overseas donors.

The CBO also has a problematic relationship to the whole issue of resource management. When the Wildlife Management Area was established, a special committee was set up as required by national legislation, to create a set of formal management rules. Once the Wildlife Management Area was legally established, this committee ceased to function but, by law, they continue to be responsible for the monitoring and enforcement of the management rules. They are also the only body with the legal authority to change those rules. The village committee appointed to set up the CBO proposed that this committee should act under the authority of the CBO Board of Directors, and that they would be re-activated once the CBO was up and running. It remains to be seen, however, whether this approach to resource management will be effective at Lababia.

Conclusion

A lack of accountability would seem to be the inevitable outcome of the ideological and institutional weaknesses of the current approach to conservation and development projects. Decision-making processes are scattered among a large and divergent group of stakeholders, whose roles and responsibilities are often poorly defined. Facilitating NGOs often lack the expertise to deliver on the development side of the conservation for development transaction that is a fundamental, ideological component of these projects. Funding insecurity puts pressure on facilitating NGOs to gather only the type of information that has promotional value within funding competitions. And finally, as a consequence of the inequalities of power that occur within current institutional arrangements, local communities often find that their interests are subordinate to those of the facilitating NGO.

As a result of these constraints, consulting anthropologists and independent researchers face serious difficulties when they set out to work in support of the broad goals of conservation and development projects. In my own case, I had gone to Lababia with the understanding that VDT were interested in the type of research information I proposed to gather. They had assisted me in setting up my research project in the village, and offered me the use of their office space while in Lae. I discovered soon after my arrival however, that their primary motivation in inviting me to Lababia lay in their desire to have a long-term, paying customer in the village guesthouse. This became evident after I discovered that the guesthouse was poorly suited to my needs, and had made arrangements to move into the village itself. Senior VDT staff members then accused me of "undermining" the guesthouse operation, and threatened to remove my office privileges. They especially wanted to have a scientist in the guesthouse, since it allowed them to claim some success in their efforts to promote the center as a research facility. Although good relations were subsequently restored, it was not until the end of my stay in Lababia, that VDT staff began to take a serious interest in the type of information I was gathering and its possible relevance to the project.[10]

Integrated conservation and development projects nevertheless represent a significant improvement over previous conservation initiatives since they recognize the rights of those communities living in and around the areas targeted for conservation initiatives. The institutional analysis presented here, however, suggests that it is not enough to simply offer local communities the chance to *participate* in project interventions. Their role should be more authoritative than that. In fact it is the external agencies that should be requesting the opportunity to *participate* in local institutions of environmental management. In this scenario external agencies become players in a community-based management system, and become a type of resource-owner in their own right. By redefining a people's traditional territory as a conservation area, these external agencies have in effect created a new resource—biodiversity itself—and are proposing to local communities that they (the agencies) should exercise custodial rights over that resource. From this perspective conservation and development organizations should quite legitimately be expected to *buy* or at least *earn* their seat at the table.

By participating in village-based decision making processes, rather than displacing such activities to distant locations, conservation and development agencies could support a process of gradual institutional innovation at the community level. Institutional innovation is one of the key mechanisms by which a community adapts to changing circumstances, and the ability to innovate effectively is a core characteristic of those common property systems that have shown themselves to be sustainable over long periods of time.

Acknowledgments

I would first like to express my gratitude to the villagers of Lababia, who generously allowed me to live in their village and carry out my research project. I am also indebted to the staff of Village Development Trust for helping me to set up my research project in Lababia, and providing me with generous access to their office space while I was in Lae. The first version of this essay was presented during an ASAO conference session on "Anthropology and Consultancy" in Vancouver in 1999, and this final version has benefited enormously from the review and feedback provided to me by Leslie Butt. Research funding was provided by the International Development Research Center of Canada, the Social Sciences and Humanities Research Council of Canada, le Fonds FCAR of the Province of Québec, and the Social Sciences and Humanities Research Grants Subcommittee of McGill University.

Notes

1. See James (1996) for a description of those projects that had been implemented prior to April 1995. More up-to-date information can be found in an upcoming publication edited by Colin Filer (n.d.).
2. See especially Oates (1999), Terborgh (1999), and van Schaik and Kramer (1997). A critical review of this literature has been written by Wilshusen et al. (2002).
3. Brown and Fox (1998) provide an excellent analysis of this problem in one chapter of a book that deals with accountability at the World Bank.
4. The village was given the name Lababia when German government officials arrived in the area in the 1890s. The name refers to the point of land where the community was then settled, whereas today their village site is located at Kamiali, 3 kilometers farther south. Villagers decided to name the project after their current place of residence, rather than use the official village name.
5. The "advocacy" approach I adopted in my doctoral studies followed on my previous work as a research consultant to aboriginal communities in British Columbia, work that included a wide range of community-based planning activities related to environment and development issues.
6. The official gazette notice describes the area as 47,413 hectares, but the area has subsequently and more accurately been calculated as 43,400 hectares (Bein 1998:10).
7. A few months after the collapse of the village fishing project, the boat and icebox were sold by VDT to a man widely regarded as the best commercial fisherman in the village. He has been far more successful than the village cooperative, but his profit margin has been too low to keep up with his monthly payments to VDT. In the eight months from December 1998 to August 1999, he grossed K7052.75 from fish sales and passenger fees, but spent in excess of K6000.00 on gas, ice, wages to assistants, and other costs. Gas costs alone ate up 46 percent of his gross income.
8. Leadership positions in Lababia are achieved according to the "great man" pattern described by Godelier (1986), and bear no relationship to the "big man" pattern as described by Strathern (1971). In this chapter I use the pidgin term *bigman*, as it is used in Lababia and generally throughout PNG, to refer to community leaders who have achieved leadership status in a wide variety of ways.
9. In the case of a similar project at Crater Mountain, West (2001) reports that project-generated income averaged K8.09 per person in 1997. By comparison, the income generated by small-holder coffee-growing operations (not a project activity) averaged K79.82 per person. Most of the project-generated income came from the sale of bilums manufactured by women. See also James (1996), who states that development has generally been "the weak link" in conservation and development projects.
10. As it turns out, the information I gathered during the course of my "voluntary" consultancy was never fully utilized by Village Development Trust, at least not to my knowledge. In the fall of 2001 I returned to PNG to present copies of my completed Ph.D. thesis

and a 30-page summary of the thesis, in pidgin, to villagers and VDT staff. I also proposed to villagers that, with their consent and advice, I would publish a shortened form of the thesis as a book. I also arranged to meet with the VDT Director of the Kamiali Project to obtain his comments and advice. Villagers set aside a whole day to discuss the content of the thesis with me, and during a protracted and heated debate, concern was expressed by some individuals about my description of clan histories. In the end, however, they approved publication of the thesis on condition that certain changes would be made. The VDT Director, on the other hand, did not find time for a substantive review of the thesis before our meeting and did not offer any constructive criticism or recommendations for changes. He did request, and I agreed, that VDT should feel free to cite passages from the thesis in future reports and grant applications. After I returned to Canada, however, and the Director found time to read the thesis in more detail, I received a repudiation, by email, of criticisms I had made of VDT's role in the project. Otherwise, I have received no feedback from VDT staff concerning the thesis, its future publication, or use. Arrangements to publish the thesis have not yet been finalized.

References

Bein, F.L. (ed) 1998 *Kamiali Wildlife Management Area Bio-Diversity Inventory*. A report prepared for Village Development Trust, Lae: The Environmental Research and Management Center, Papua New Guinea University of Technology.

Brown, L.D. and Jonathan A. Fox 1998 "Accountability within Transnational Coalitions". In Jonathan A. Fox and L.D. Brown (eds) *The Struggle for Accountability: The World Bank, NGOs, and Grassroots Movements*, pp. 439–483. Cambridge, Mass.: The MIT Press.

Brown, M. and B. Wyckoff 1992 *Designing Integrated Conservation and Development Projects*. Washington, D.C.: Biodiversity Support Program/United States Agency of International Development (USAID).

Filer, Colin (ed) n.d. *Custom, Conservation, and Development in Papua New Guinea*. Canberra: Resource Management in Asia-Pacific Project, Research School of Pacific and Asian Studies, Australian National University (forthcoming).

Godelier, Maurice 1986 *The Making of Great Men: Male Domination and Power Among the New Guinea Baruya*. Cambridge: Cambridge University Press.

James, Jamie (ed) 1996 *Proceedings of the 1995 Meeting of Integrated Conservation and Development Projects in Papua New Guinea*. Port Moresby: Papua New Guinea Department of Environment and Conservation, and United Nations Development Programme.

Margoluis, Richard and Nick Salafsky 1998 *Measures of Success: Designing, Managing, and Monitoring Conservation and Development Projects*. Washington, D.C.: Island Press.

Martin, R. E. 1998 "Integrating Conservation and Development in a Papua New Guinean Community: Kamiali—a Case Study". Ph.D. diss., Department of Geography and Environmental Science, Melbourne: Monash University.

McCallum, Rob and Nikhil Sekhran 1997 *Race for the Rainforest: Evaluating Lessons from an Integrated Conservation and Development 'Experiment' in New Ireland, Papua New Guinea*. Waigani, Papua New Guinea: PNG Biodiversity Conservation and Resource Management Programme.

Oates, J. F. 1999 *Myth and Reality in the Rain Forest: How Conservation Strategies Are Failing in West Africa*, Berkeley: University of California Press.

Ostrom, Elinor 1990 *Governing the Commons: The Evolution of Institutions for Collective Action*. Cambridge: Cambridge University Press.

———— 1992 "The Rudiments of a Theory of the Origins, Survival, and Performance of Common-Property Institutions". In D.W. Bromley (ed) *Making the Commons Work: Theory, Practice, and Policy*, pp. 293–318. San Francisco: ICS Press.

Pinkerton, Evelyn and Martin Weinstein 1995 *Fisheries That Work: Sustainability Through Community-Based Management*. Vancouver: The David Suzuki Foundation.

Sekhran, N. and S. Miller 1994 *Papua New Guinea Country Study on Biological Diversity*. A report to the United Nations Environment Program, Waigani, Papua New Guinea: The Conservation Resource Centre of the Papua New Guinea Department of Environment and Conservation, and the Africa Centre for Resources and Environment (ACRE).

Shaw, Mike 1999 Personal communication. Lae, Papua New Guinea, July 25, 1999.

Strathern, Andrew 1971 *The Rope of Moka: Big Men and Ceremonial Exchange in Mount Hagen*. Cambridge: Cambridge University Press.

Terborgh, J. 1999 *Requiem for Nature*. Washington, D.C.: Island Press/Shearwater Books.

van Helden, Flip n.d. "The Community Entry Approach of the Bismarck-Ramu Integrated Conservation and Development Project". In Colin Filer (ed) *Custom, Conservation, and Development in Papua New Guinea*, chap. 6. Canberra: Resource Management in Asia-Pacific Project, Research School of Pacific and Asian Studies, Australian National University (forthcoming).

van Schaik, C.P. and R.A. Kramer 1997 "Towards a New Protectionist Paradigm". In R.A. Kramer, C.P. van Schaik, and J. Johnson (eds) *Last Stand: Protected Areas and the Defense of Tropical Biodiversity*, pp. 212–230. New York: Oxford University Press.

Wade, Robert 1988 *Village Republics: Economic Conditions for Collective Action in South India*. Cambridge: Cambridge University Press.

Wells, M. and K. Brandon 1992 *People and Parks: Linking Protected Area Management with Local Communities*. Washington, D.C.: The World Bank.

West, Paige n.d. "The Unintended Social Consequences of Conservation in Maimafu Village". In C. Filer (ed) *Custom, Conservation, and Development in Papua New Guinea*, chap. 4. Canberra: Resource Management in Asia-Pacific Project, Research School of Pacific and Asian Studies, Australian National University (forthcoming).

Wilshusen, P.R., S.R. Brechin, C.L. Fortwangler, and P.C. West 2002 "Reinventing a Square Wheel: Critique of a Resurgent 'Protection Paradigm' in International Biodiversity Conservation". *Society and Natural Resources* 15(1):17–40.

Chapter 5

WHERE ANTHROPOLOGISTS FEAR TO TREAD
Notes and Queries on Anthropology and Consultancy, Inspired by a Fieldwork Experience

Lorenzo Brutti

In this essay I give an account of my experience of almost a year of survey work as a consultant for a mining company whose presence affected the population I studied as an anthropologist, the Oksapmin of Sandaun Province in Papua New Guinea.

Before approaching the ethnographic description of the survey together with my method of working, I will discuss the main issues which encompass the work of the anthropologist. I am especially interested in the stage when the researcher switches from the role of the ethnographer, aiming to carry out scientific work, to that of the consultant, which is—by definition—more embedded in economic and political matters.

I share in its entirety Colin Filer's position: " *this particular setting* is one in which it *normally* does make more sense for anthropologists to act as 'honest brokers' in mediating the relationships between different stakeholders (including the multi-national companies) than it does to act as the partisans or the advocates of local communities in their struggle against the 'world capitalist system'" (Filer 1999:89). Also, because local communities are often struggling not only against the 'world capitalist system' but also against other globalized ideological systems, as they perceive these, the anthropologist should take this into serious account since he or she is engaged in more than a cold and professional work of consultancy. I refer to all the kinds of ideological and contemporary religious patterns which may interact with the work of anthropologist in several ways.

There are some fundamental differences between fieldwork as an ethnographer and fieldwork as a consultant, which the anthropologist switching to the role of consultant will necessarily experience. I will mention the most

Notes for this chapter are located on page 122.

evident of these or, at least, those which were the most visible to me in my experience as a consultant.

The main difference that appeared to me concerned the focus of the research. When you are in the field for your "classic" academic work, preparing a Ph.D., or during one of your several fieldwork trips in the context of your scientific study, you have much more flexible aims. You are free to choose and determine your topic of interest and to deal with it by exercising a certain degree of freedom within the limits of time and of the funding you have for your study.

In the context of a consultancy, you are "framed" in different ways. You are given a topic of research by your employer and you can choose to take it up or not, but there is very little you can do to modify the topic itself within the frame of the consultancy. Often the issue is "take it or leave it". Even though you accept the contract hoping to carry out some work which will also coincide with your own interests, at the end of the contract you must produce a report and give the results of the survey as it was commanded by the hiring company. Of course, the same conclusion is requested of the ethnographer in an academic context, but there the possibilities of action are much greater. We can switch from one topic to another if we realize that our original topic—decided at our desk at home—does not fit with the reality of fieldwork. We can also normally ask for additional time if the conduct of our research is more complicated and longer than expected. I would call this option the "liberty to choose the research topic" which is common in academic fieldwork whereas consultancy topics are not chosen by the ethnographer but simply accepted or refused.

Therefore, one of the first problems the ethnographer must consider in approaching a proposition for a consultancy is the feasibility and the pertinence of the topic together with a precise estimation of the time given to produce the report on that particular topic. This may seem relatively easy for an ethnographer who is a specialist on the area in which he/she is requested to do the survey, but the evaluation of difficulties within the fieldwork in relation to the requested topic and the schedule of the tasks to complete the job can be more complicated than expected.

Along with this matter concerning the freedom of choice of the ethnographic topic, we can consider the opposition between academic and consultancy ethnography or, in a broader sense, the opposition between public and private studies. By contrast with a classic ethnographic study—which is due to be published and diffused—often the results of the consultancy survey are requested by the employer to be confidential, at least for a certain time. Here is a first matter of engagement and ethical approach toward the local people. Why should the social actors of the survey not know the results of the study in which they stand as the main characters? This is hopefully not often the case, but in several consultancies the results or a part of them are confidential and not published, either in specialized journals or in local magazines.

But the main issue concerning the anthropologist, who might be doubtful about accepting or refusing the enterprise of a consultancy asked for by a foreign private company on the society he/she already knows as an ethnographer, is mainly a matter of ethics. It is hard to generalize about this problem, but consultancies often are requested by foreign private companies and often concern the financial interests of those corporations. It may be that these interests do not always fit or benefit the local population. But in the end, the anthropologist is forced to choose between doing the job himself/herself or letting it go to another consultant who might not know the fieldwork area with the same depth as an ethnographer who has spent a considerable amount of time with the population concerned. In this last case, the less dangerous decision, at least for the society which is the focus of the survey, is that the anthropologist will be the consultant, even though for the anthropologist personally it is often not professionally prestigious to accept a consultancy. Indeed, in the European academic milieu, there is a tendency to look at consultancy work as a faulty practice aimed at acquiring monetary pay for the researcher's competencies. This is true at least in Europe and in the countries like France that have a Catholic tradition as opposed to the Protestant-based countries, where the relationship between academics and monetary rewards is much less charged with guilt and is more equilibrated. Often, within this historical and cultural background, the work of an academic as a consultant is at best not perceived as scientific—because in it not enough purely "scientific" work is done. In the worst case, to accept to work in a consultancy is seen as a sort of scientific prostitution for an academic.

This is an endogenous problem which the anthropologist has to deal with in his/her academic environment. Another problem the anthropologist has to deal with is of an exogenous kind, and is related to his/her informants, with the society he/she knows as an ethnographer and where he/she would probably entertain good relationships and continue to carry out fieldwork for years. This is a very delicate matter because the anthropologist has to be aware that, because he/she is working for a company, the population will sooner or later assimilate the researcher to the company directing the survey. At that stage all the responsibilities of the company will be imputed to the anthropologist. The consultant will then have a hard time in trying to redefine the respective responsibilities, stressing the differences between an occasional individual employment—probably accepted with the aim of honestly helping the people in doing the job as well as possible—and an overall policy of profit managed by a multi-national mining company.

Concerning the rationalization the anthropologist could make of the needs of the local people, this is often a matter of mistaken Western-oriented ecological interpretations. It is my personal experience that the ecological preoccupation of the Oksapmin was and still is absolutely far from that of a European ethno-ecologist such as myself at the time of the survey.

I have not found any emic discourse about long-term environmental management. The Oksapmin profess their right to exploit their environment, to "eat" their river and the surrounding forest environment. Their discourse addressed to me as a mediator between them and the company may have been aimed at helping them to take profit from the situation and to "exploit" the company without being very critical of it. They feared that if they acted in an ecologically critical way, the company might give up, and together with the company the chance of enrichment and development would have been lost.

It is absolutely true that, for the most remote hamlets of the Oksapmin area, where there are water tanks or a regular distribution of medicines, the company does this and not the State of Papua New Guinea, which does not have the financial capacity to do it. It is therefore comprehensible that a majority of people are positive in regard to the presence of the company.

Finally, what should an anthropologist do in such a situation? Fight against the windmills hoping that the companies may be overcome? Probably no anthropologist seriously hopes this may ever be possible. I think instead the strategy may be the one of the Trojan horse, and that the anthropologist may be more useful to the local people as Ulysses rather than as Don Quixote. Of course, the anthropologist must do a lot of previous work together with the local people to try to fully understand their needs, and perhaps give advice to re-orient them. Such a kind of approach may be more helpful than an international court case, because once the anthropologist is inside the mechanism he/she is perceived as an interlocutor rather than as an adversary and, as an interlocutor, he/she has much more negotiating power with the company.

The Survey

Porgera Joint Venture (hereafter PJV) is a mining company located an hour's flight away from Oksapmin. Nevertheless, the effects of the operation are visible in Oksapmin territory: 17,000 tons of stones and earth together with chemical waste products of the gold cleaning process are thrown every day in the waters of the Strickland-Lagaip riverine system of the region. This ecological impact is argued by some parties to have provoked chemical pollution and sedimentation and erosion of the riverbanks. After an agreement signed with the Government of Papua New Guinea, the company was required to compensate the local population, affected by these ecological changes, for its use of the river to dispose of mine tailings. It was further required, by mining law, to sponsor a local survey of the kind I was asked to undertake.

When I arrived in Porgera in February 1998, I had an incomplete idea of the purpose of the survey I was asked to do. I was contacted by PJV in 1997 and asked to carry out a genealogical and topographical survey of five villages of the Strickland-Lagaip basin. That communication did not mention the exact aim of the study, which I eventually learned to be the payment for the water use permit to the people living on the Strickland-Lagaip waterfront. That is why it took me a few days after my arrival to understand what was demanded of me as an anthropological specialist of the area.

The area I was asked to study comprised the Dubanap, Kunanap, Gaua, and Sanapte villages of the Oksapmin area, the Gapka and Sungtem villages of the Bimin area, and the Sisimin and Nene villages of the Hewa area.

In my understanding, the main concerns of PJV in the frame of the Strickland-Lagaip survey were the following:

- to ascertain the clan boundaries along the river system territories of the villages;
- to study and register them on a topographic map in order to calculate the amount of money to be paid to each clan;
- to identify trustworthy landowners as agents to deal directly with the company during the payment;
- to identify suitable services and other kinds of help that might in general be sponsored or promoted by the company in the villages concerned.

Method of Survey

In carrying out my fieldwork I adopted the classic ethnographic method of directed interviews and participatory observation. A series of large audience interviews concerned clan boundaries along the river, the ecological use and spiritual importance of the river, settlement and migration patterns on the basin, requests to the company in terms of finances and services, and selection of agents.

Restricted interviews concerned secret histories about mythical origins of clans and elements of oral tradition that testified to the ownership of land by a given clan.

Direct observation concerned village infrastructures for development (where existing), the recording of clan boundaries, and the identification of leaders and remarkable persons. Topics of a confidential kind included counseling on positive or negative individuals with whom I dealt in the frame of the survey and who might be future collaborators or opponents in relations between the mine company and the indigenous community.

Census data were collected directly on the house location with specific interviews, one for each household, or, more often, were given by the householder or by another member of the household to the anthropologist. The census field was established on the basis of the information PJV required. Moreover, an accurate demographic chart of the region surveyed was especially useful for establishing health and educational infrastructure as well as other kind of services such as water provision, bridges, and airstrips.

Most of the boundaries survey was carried out by aerial (helicopter) GPS recordings shared, guided, and witnessed by traditional landowners.

The landowners were indicated by the people themselves and the anthropologist made a final selection of one or more landowners within each clan to carry out the helicopter survey.

During the village fieldwork several days were spent in public discussions about significant elements in oral tradition establishing the traditional land ownership of each clan. Most of the landowners were very comfortable and prompt in indicating the boundaries of their clan.

My technique for approaching the population of each village visited and explaining the reasons my presence and my work there was to organize a big meeting the day following my arrival. That public meeting was held—wherever possible—in the lingua franca, Tok Pisin, by myself, or in vernacular language through the help of an indigenous mother-tongue translator. The aim of the meeting was to announce to the people the meaning of my presence there and the job I was going to do with their help. I always insisted as much as possible on the difference between my own previous work as an ethnographer and the operation carried out for the company. That is why I preferred not to be assisted by any other company worker, in order to avoid misunderstandings. The people knew me as an anthropologist before my engagement with PJV on the survey. On the basis of my relationship with the people, I tried to avoid misunderstanding about my role. I explained as accurately as I could the meaning of the survey and why PJV had asked me to carry it out as an anthropologist and specialist of the area. As far as possible I avoided talking about technical matters concerning the company's policies which were not within my competence.

My field assistants handled the work of translation during the interviews with elders who did not speak Tok Pisin.

The Oksapmin

The 10,137[1] Oksapmin live at between 1,500 and 2,200 meters elevation in the high valleys of Trangap, Tekin, Gaua, Bak, and Kwiva in Sandaun Province, in a territory covering a surface of approximately 1,000 square kilometers. The population density for the main valley of Trangap is 16 inhabitants per square kilometer, but it becomes sensibly lower away from the main settlement area. A limited but quite good diffusion of monetarization for such an isolated area allows Oksapmin people to use planes quite often as a means of transport. Two airstrips have been opened in the area: Oksapmin airstrip in the main valley of Trangap and Tekin airstrip,

in the Tekin valley beside the Australian Baptist Mission. Thanks to monetarization and aerial links, Oksapmin young and married men are used
to traveling quite often to urban centers (Tabubil, Hagen, Port Moresby,
etc.) for working or occasional trips.

Oksapmin are sedentary horticulturists. Hunting and gathering have
now a decreasing importance in the people's diet compared to pre-contact
times. The main staple is sweet potato (*Ipomoea batatas*). Vegetables are
cultivated for marketing mainly at the Tabubil mine center by the indigenous co-operative Oksapmin Vegetable Market. The sale of these products
represents a significant source of income for the Oksapmin people.

Evangelization started when the Australian Baptist Mission settled in
Oksapmin in 1961. Before that date Oksapmin people had no regular contacts with Westerners.[2] The monetarization process began in Oksapmin
during the 1970s through outgoing laborers moving toward the coastal
copra and coffee plantations. Nowadays, several Oksapmin, mainly men,
are employed by the mining companies settled in the area, especially Ok
Tedi Mining Limited (OTML). Tabubil, the base of the OTML, is today the
most important mine center, whose population is partly composed of
hundreds of informal residents, relatives of the mine workers coming
from Oksapmin.

The Oksapmin social structure is hard to define in classic anthropological terms. Clans are the fundamental units of the Oksapmin social structure even though there is no direct term for "clan" in the Oksapmin
language. About 50 clans exist in the five Oksapmin valleys. It is hard to
fit the Oksapmin social organization in any single one of the classic kinship categories. The Oksapmin clan is an exogamous unilineal descent
group, but it acts more as a cognatic group in matters of land inheritance.
It is forbidden to marry inside the same clan and a new couple may go to
cultivate the land of the bride's parents. Belonging to a given clan means
to become part of an internal network of social solidarity concretized by
mutual help. The most important characteristic of the Oksapmin clan is its
specialization in specific traditional competencies concerning the managing of animals (possums, pigs, cassowaries) and the evocation of natural
phenomena (earthquake, wind, rain, etc.). A clan is said to have originated from a *mongsup*, a chthonian spirit (animal, vegetal, mineral, or
pseudo-human) who gave birth to the first lineages of the clan's human
ancestors. An original clan may split into several lineages through changes
in residential patterns of its segments. The whole Oksapmin society is
acephalous, but each clan has ritual specialists (*aw äm hän*) and traditional
leaders (*kak hän*) who make decisions about land use within clan territories. The *kak hän* were my privileged interlocutors in dealing with matters
concerning the definition of clan boundaries and compensation.

There is a continuity concerning the mode of succession to leadership
over time since in Oksapmin pre-contact society leadership was held by
ritual specialists, and nowadays the leadership is held by men who have

a role to play in the main contemporary issues which are the concern of the churches. Local pastors, who are indeed quite often the sons of former traditional leaders, are today the most important persons. This does not means that power and leadership are hereditary, but the son of an important man is supposed to carry on the work of his father. If he is unable to do that, the vacant position will be filled by a new, young, brilliant "self-made" man. Given that the Australian government stopped warfare in the region in the early 1960s and that the Protestant and Seventh-day Adventist Churches began to forbid any form of traditional ceremony in the same years, the traditional Oksapmin form of leadership has found a new venue in the newly imported political and religious patterns.

The last initiation ceremonies took place in 1960; since then, they have been stopped by the active disapproval of the Australian Baptist Mission, which still continues (Peter Gay, ABMS, pers.com., September 1996). These ritual activities were fundamental for cultural transmission. Because of the abandoning of these practices, Oksapmin culture has changed deeply and has lost its traditional, pre-contact significance. In a few decades, when the whole cohort of the initiated men will be deceased, there will be no more people able to transmit the ecological knowledge concerning the environment which was encapsulated within ritual action. Unfortunately, that period will coincide with the end of the mine company's operations around the Oksapmin region. At that time an important number of mine workers will probably have to go back to live in the village and base their economy on agro-forestry. Those people will not have the ecological competence of their grandfathers.

There were in Oksapmin traditional forms of behavior consciously directed toward the maintenance of natural land resources: hunting magic, pandanus magic and a paramount ritual of fertility called *yuan-hän* based on human sacrifice (Brutti 1997). All of these customs have been abandoned. There were also traditional forms of behavior which had the unintended effect of conserving natural resources on land such as the taboos on cutting trees around pandanus plants or on killing certain animals or eating the fruits of certain bush trees. People recognize different types of sacred sites (*awam ap* or *awam mong*): ceremonial houses, mythical trackways, and sites related to the *yuan hän* ritual. Several of those sacred sites are located on the Strickland-Lagaip riverbanks.

People are nowadays officially converted to the Christian religion and they perceive the traditional religion as evil. The ceremonial houses were destroyed during the process of evangelization and the portions of forest which were forbidden for gardening in the past are now being cultivated. From the people's point of view there is little concern about environmental protection concerning the forest, whereas the river basin environment is considered to be in danger because of erosion and chemical pollution.

There are differences between the elder and younger generations when talking about development, but these are not as important as the differences between men and women when talking about the same topic. The discourse about development is oriented by gender in Oksapmin, in the sense that it is mainly held by men, not by women. This is a consequence of the prevalent male bias in education and migration. Women have not migrated as workers and there are no women with university degrees and very few with high school certificates in Oksapmin. Another reason is related to the gendered division of labor. Because of male out-migration often the women of a family have had to take charge of garden and forest activities. Consequently, for the village women the coming of development has not changed their working life. What has changed is the women's role in religious behavior and, gradually, in social life. With an increasing emphasis on the nuclear family as opposed to the traditional extended family based on patrilocal patterns, some women, although not all, have acquired more influence over their husbands than these men's brothers or male relatives have in decisions regarding the use of forest resources. The influence consists in pushing the husband toward a decision between several possibilities, but women do not have the opportunity to make their own decisions concerning forested land. There are no women's organizations.

The most important agents of communication through whom the idea of 'sustainable development' has entered the community have been outside workers, students and politicians. Mainly men between 20 and 40 years, working and living, alone or together with their families, in the mine centers compose the first category of agents, the migrants. They play a role of information and updating, and they are the main link between the village community and the urban, developed context. Women are included in this category, as the sisters, wives, mothers, or daughters of the mine workers, often living with them or visiting their relatives in town for several weeks, sometimes for months. Nevertheless, their role is less important than that of their male relatives.

The second category is the high school, college, or university students. They are young people, male and female, between 15 and 25 years old, living in coastal towns such as Vanimo or Lae. They are the most recent category of educated people. They are cultivated, so they have competence and knowledge about development.

The third category is the most powerful in terms of influence. To this category belong the provincial and national politicians. They are all adult men, all initiated, who have lived through a fundamental historical and cultural process, in the pre-contact era and the coming of evangelization and the colonial protectorate administration until independence. They are competent in—and they benefit from—both the traditional customs and the globalization process. They went through initiation and they know the traditional knowledge of their culture (which gives them a power similar to that of the *kak hän*, the traditional leaders) and they have been educated in missionary and government schools.

Information about governmental policy is obtained by the Officer in Charge and by the local politicians. Small-scale government projects have undertaken the regeneration of limited areas of anthropogenic grassland. Inspired by governmental examples, Oksapmin people have learned to plant *Casuarina* sp. trees. Apart from that there is no special spontaneous concern about sustainable development. The most common expressions for 'sustainable development' are idioms meaning help coming from national institutions in which sustaining is still conceived of as unilateral assistance.

For example, the obligation to pay taxes to government is generally avoided. This could be partly justified by the absence or the inefficiency of governmental services. The Oksapmin Patrol Post, started in 1961, has been unofficially closed during the last five years. The public servants are not motivated in their work, they have very poor equipment, and they are often paid only after several months of delay. Because of these reasons, when people talk about government, the feeling is one of being betrayed. Moreover, there is a common suspicion that government or big religious organizations such as the Catholic Church will come to Oksapmin to steal the land from the people (Brutti 1999). As a result of all these concomitant causes, people in the Lagaip-Strickland area do not want any involvement from the government on the customary land; they prefer to deal with private companies. They are especially interested in relations with mining companies, because they know private companies pay well and regularly. People do not care too much about environmental conservation policy. It seems that they do not believe that land resources are limited in space and time, also because historically there is no similar situation in the past with which they can compare the present.

Conversion, Cultural Change, and Cosmology

As among the other Ok people, there is no antinomy among the Oksapmin between two different universes, the human one, represented by human culture and society, and the environmental one, formed by natural, non-human beings. In the Oksapmin language, as in many other New Guinea languages, there are no words for "religion". The idea of a relation with transcendental beings, either spirits (e.g. *mongsup* which means ground spirit) or deities (e.g. *yuan*) is not a concept separated from the natural universe. Every activity inside the human or the natural environment is embedded in the sphere of religion and ritual.

In the transition from the "traditional" cosmology to the imported one—the process of conversion to Christianity—what is changing is the paradigm of reference even though certain modes of expression remain apparently unaltered. In the case of Oksapmin cosmological ideas, the transition to Christianity was a shift from a polymorphic pantheon dominated by Yuan (Afek in Telefol), the paramount female spirit, to a similar ecocosmological milieu conquered by the introduced Christian God. The polytheistic and more archaic reference, represented by the spirit panoply, has remained almost unaltered. The ground spirits (*mongsup*) are still held to exist and continue their work and this is also the case in other Ok groups converted to Christianity. Sorcery (*tam äm*) is still a matter of actuality in contemporary Oksapmin society. People nowadays go to church but still tend to impute any accident, injury, or anomaly occurring in the normal course of social and natural life to sorcery. In Oksapmin culture, sorcery has endogenous causes. The guilty must always be found inside the victim's clan. Village courts are frequently held to discuss sorcery cases.

Applying this point in the ecological dimension, it is possible to see how cosmogonic representations have influenced ecological praxis. As has already been stressed, Christianity has inculcated the concept of the: "human dominion over the earth and its fruits, the familiar Christian idea of the human domination of nature.... They are free to take from nature what they want and to consume it as they want" (Robbins 1995:215–217).

The conversion to the Christian religion has conduced to opening a gap between the people and their ecological environment. The people feel free to use the ecological landscape, the forest environment, to show that they have abandoned the ancestors' fallacious beliefs and they are following the right way of Christianity.

What, then, does religious change have to do with consultancy and particularly with the social and genealogical survey on which I was employed as an anthropologist? The overall answer is that Oksapmin society is characterized by important socio-economic change, and people are trying to use their religious framework as a way to resolve social conflicts. In a certain sense, most of the new Christian adepts in Oksapmin are the product of the first acculturated generation. These are people who have been integrated into the world of schools, stores, and salaries. They have internalized capitalistic-oriented representations about development and are potentially in a position of crisis or even of subjection, in social and economic terms. Having entered the process of globalization, they are conscious that they are citizens of a country with important social, economic and political problems, compared to countries that are often seen as referential models of efficiency (e.g. Australia, the U.S.). This cultural representation shows us how much religious discourse is embedded in political values.

Why are the facts relating to Oksapmin traditional cosmological rituals so important in the contemporary ecological and political issues? How can ancient beliefs affect the way in which people create current representations of PJV's presence and impact on the river system?

The first remark is of a topographical kind. In the Oksapmin mythical and historical times, innovation came from the east, from the Highlands through the Strickland, following the sunrise. This was the case for the cosmological renewal brought by Yuan (Afek), the "big mother" of all Min people. This was also the case for the introduction of the sweet potato, which arrived in the Oksapmin areas from the Highlands through the Strickland. It was, further, the case of the first white man[3] who penetrated the area coming from the Highlands and crossing the Strickland. Later, in the 1960s, the first missions which settled in the area had their headquarters in Mount Hagen, also to the east.

Each upheaval in Oksapmin history came from the Highlands side through the Strickland. This is important in order to understand why the effects of PJV's operations on the Strickland river system had such a big impact on the cultural representations concerning the environment.

This is not the first case of a mining company presence in the wider area. Since the early 1980s, people were used to witnessing the impact in the area to their west of a big mining company, Ok Tedi Mining. The erosion of a cultural landscape like the one provoked by Ok Tedi Mining Ltd. (OTML) on Mount Fubilan has, however, affected the Oksapmin people much less than the impact of PJV on the Strickland. Of course, there are practical reasons for this, related to geographical proximity. Mount Fubilan in the Tabubil area is far from Oksapmin territories. The difference in the impact between OTML and PJV in the Oksapmin ecological landscape is due to the fact that Mt Fubilan is a ten days' walk from Oksapmin and it is not part of the Oksapmin territory, but the Strickland river "belongs" to the Oksapmin who can witness every day its changes in colour, erosion, depth and other phenomenological aspects. The pollution and erosion of the Strickland riverine system by tailings from Porgera show visible effects right in the Oksapmin area. The complaints of the local people against the Porgera company were not only expressed in terms of material, ecological impact, but also in terms of the profanation of sacred sites and perturbation of a cosmic order. The river always had a cosmological value in Oksapmin culture. In Oksapmin narrative there is no origin myth of the Strickland like that for the Lagaip in the Hewa myths, but the river is always a central element in the traditional narratives.

The Strickland is believed to be the origin of wild pigs. A mythical animal called *sip* generated the wild pigs. This mythical animal is described as a quadruped the size of a cow and it is sometimes called "water buffalo". This appellation could be misleading. People say that the *sip* did not have horns like a buffalo, but he had tusks like wild pigs. Archaeological and zoological data lead us to advance the hypothesis that the idea of the *sip* may be the oral reminiscence of an extinct marsupial, *Huliterium thomasettii*. This mythical animal was the "father" of wild pigs, the spirit who originated wild pigs.

People now say that chemical pollution is the reason why wild pigs down at the Strickland riverbank grassland area are so scarce nowadays and that the mine's activities have killed the *sip*. People want to be compensated not only for the ecological impact of PJV's presence in the area but more importantly for the profanation of the sacred spirits and the violation of ritual sites. It might be objected that contemporary evangelized Oksapmin people do not follow ancient rituals and do not any longer believe in traditional cosmology. But the contemporary situation in Oksapmin is much more complex, and it cannot be reduced to the dualistic opposition of present/past or traditional beliefs/evangelization. As I have explained in the presentation of traditional fertility ritual, the conversion to Western religion has been a superficial process, materially oriented, through which the traditional cosmological infrastructure has been consciously removed in order to introduce the new beliefs. The traditional beliefs have not entirely disappeared. They have been hidden from sight of the pastors and the "white men" in general, who were supposed to follow the same corpus of religious tradition. Practices of sorcery, witchcraft, divination and garden magic are still alive since they have a deep existence in social and cultural history and they cannot be washed away in a couple of generations. If the ceremonial and spirit houses have been rushed away under the pressure of missionaries, if the initiations have been forbidden, this only represents the tip of the iceberg which has been leveled to the surface. An enormous corpus of traditional beliefs is still going on in everyday life. This cultural heritage has not been erased by a forced process of conversion in a couple of decades. It has just been modulated and adapted to the changed external constraints owing to the arrival of the new cosmology of Christianity.

That is why the spiritual significance of the Lagaip and Strickland rivers in indigenous culture had to be taken into account and people had to be compensated for their perceptions of ecological as well as of cultural damages.

Chemical pollution, according to the people, killed the "wild pig's father" whereas the erosion had washed away the signs of the passage of the "great mother". Indeed, I have previously explained that the river was the most important part of the mythical trackway of Afek. She arrived in Oksapmin by crossing the Strickland and it was on the riverbanks that people started the cyclical *yuan-hän* ritual to thank Afek (Yuan) for having civilized them. Several ritual sites whose function is secret have been washed away by the erosion.

As a further example, fishing by hook was traditionally a secret ritual in Oksapmin carried out by initiated men. This ritual was taught to boys during the initiations. Several clans living close to the riverbanks specialized in this kind of sacral fishing. On an ethnonymic level in Oksapmin there is a general distinction between people living close to the river banks and more distant ones living up in the mountains. The people of Kunanap, Duban, and Sisimin are called *Umhän* (literally, "people who live down below"), whereas the mountain people are called *Ashän* (literally, "people who live on the top"). The difference is verbalized mainly with regard to access to different natural resources. The *Umhän* people have fruit pandanus, cassowaries, wild pigs, wild fowl and fish. The *Ashän* people have nut pandanus and possums. Only the *Umhän* people or the related clans were able to perform magic fishing by using hooks. Someone said that during the 1960s Oksapmin elders witnessed patrol officers and policemen fishing by hook along the riverbanks in front of women and children, and they were scared about the breaking of this secret knowledge.

The fish meat was traditionally prepared and consumed in sacred earth oven cookings. The fish bones were used in magic to make domestic pigs grow fat. Once more, fish, a constitutive element of the riverine ecosystem, were ritually used in relation with constitutive elements of subsistence in the land such as pig raising. People complain that chemical pollution has killed the fish, which were used to give power and health to domestic pigs.

Finally, the whole of the pig population has been symbolically affected by riverine impact. The father of the wild pigs, the *sip* spirit, has died and the wild pigs are not around the Strickland anymore. The magic essences of wealth of domestic pigs, the fish bones, have been killed by the chemical pollution and the domestic pigs do not look healthy nowadays.

Considering all those damages one may think that the ecological impact on the river may be exploited to justify most of the problems in the Strickland basin. This is not the whole case, however, because we also have to think about the ecological impact of PJV's operation on the Lagaip-Strickland riverine system in the frame of larger negative expectancies about the end of the world.

We have to analyze the local people's negative perception of the Strickland in the frame of adopted millenarian beliefs following which it is thought that the world will end with the switch to the new millennium. In this point of view, each empirically evident ecological modification is also interpreted on an ideological plane. This has been the case for large-scale phenomena such as the 1997 drought period, but also for local scale disasters such as the 1998 Aitape tidal-wave on the northern coast of Papua New Guinea, which some people saw as a punishment from God. Lagaip-Strickland pollution and erosion are also seen in ideological and cosmological terms.

Conclusions: Consultancy as Opportunity and as Dilemma

I would like to end this essay with some reflections on my own role as a consultant for a mining company who came back to work in a community which he had formerly studied as an anthropologist.

I did hesitate in accepting to carry out the survey. I accepted mainly for two reasons. First, the people were quite enthusiastic for me to be the mediator between the Oksapmin community and the company, and it was for me a further opportunity to carry out another long period of fieldwork.

The second reason that convinced me was that, if I did not accept, the survey would be carried out by some other person, who might have less knowledge of Oksapmin society or who might have less concern with the people's issues.

The position in my mind was clear from the beginning: I would have to act in the interest of the Oksapmin community as a whole and, if needed, against the interest of the company and against the interest of some few important Oksapmin persons trying to take advantage of a given situation. This is in fact what I have done. I do not pretend to be in the right. My idea of the general interest of Oksapmin society is, without any doubt, culturally and historically determined and it would probably look wrong to some at present or become obsolete in a few years. I felt myself engaged as an individual. After having spent years in Oksapmin taking benefits from my research and consequently for my scientific career, I had the opportunity to do something for the people, because the people were asking me to do it. Adventitiously, this was also an opportunity to spend some months in the field. Moreover, the people were, and still are, enthusiastic regarding the installation of private companies in their territory. Mining companies bring a flush of cash money and a network of infrastructures that the national government can hardly provide. Nowadays, what people ask for in Oksapmin is to deal with private companies either in term of compensation or in terms of negotiations for future company activities. However, I maintained that the company's role was not only to financially compensate for ecological damages but also to restore people's hope in the near future.

This does not mean that people are not concerned with the ecological impact of the mine's presence. The negative representation of the impact of PJV operations on the riverine ecosystem encompasses not just the tangible ecological damages provoked by the mining operations but also the gradual erosion of a cultural landscape and, more generally, the whole ground in a cosmological sense. In people's contemporary representations the ecological damages to the Strickland ecosystem are inscribed in the wider frame of the world's end. This is the millenarian representation predicted by most of the contemporary Melanesian churches. To respect, to understand and to accept the people's perceptions is hard for anthropologists and even harder for multi-national companies. These ecocosmological representations are not seriously understood by the mining companies and are hardly taken in account. This is a confrontation between different cultures, different cosmologies, and different economic interests.

In this sense, one of my biggest difficulties was to deal with the diffusion of census figures. I carried out, as requested by the company, a detailed census of each household filled with names, age, initiation degree, school degree, number of gardens, type, numbers and kinds of animal stock of each household. The anthropologist familiar with newly evangelized Melanesian communities will know the negative representations certain churches have of the Catholic Church, which is said to be led by the Pope/Antichrist preparing the conquest of the world. In this sense my census figures were perceived by the Oksapmin as a possible tool to help the Antichrist to exterminate their Oksapmin community. Even though I did not believe this representation, nevertheless, the conviction was fundamentally important for most of the Oksapmin community. I was dealing with a big issue, uncertain whether to respond to the people's request or to fill exactly the duties the company expected of me. Under pressure, in respect to the local people and to my own commitment with them, I decided not to include this detailed information in my report. The main issue of the survey was to produce an accurate map of the clan boundaries, which I produced in detail. Concerning the census figures, I put in my report only the general quantitative figures by village, which I thought would be enough to help the company's operations in the area. I did not enclose the specific, individual data. Of course, this decision was quite hard to undertake and I am still not sure I acted in the right way, but I was split between a professional and a community commitment. I opted for the second, deciding to satisfy the people's request of privacy and my own sense of commitment to them.

From the ethnographer's point of view, once I accepted to carry out the survey, the perception of my presence in the field as a company consultant was, of course, quite different from my previous presence as an anthropologist. But, in terms of my knowledge of the Oksapmin culture, people also asked me not to reveal certain details in my report.

In a broader sense, the positive side of having worked on this survey was to have access to the whole population whose representatives started to come to look for me and to give me a lot of information. This was an opportunity I never had previously as an anthropologist. Concerning the diffusion of my findings for the survey, the company did not forbid me to publish a part of that information under the form of anthropological papers, since it was not protected by professional secrecy.

The negative side was that, every time there was a problem with the company, I was seen as a company worker and asked to do things which were of course not in my competence nor within my responsibility. Since that was my last long period of fieldwork (nine months), I think I am still seen as a company worker by the people who know me less well, and I will never have the possibility to change this kind of representation in people's minds. Oksapmin is populated by more than 10,000 people. I know well about a hundred persons of the parishes where I have carried out my fieldwork. They know what I am interested in and what kind of work I do as an anthropologist. But the other thousands of people with whom I talked and who observed me during the long months of my consultancy will always look at me as a mine worker. And if something goes wrong with the system of compensation, they will probably think of me as sharing a part of the responsibility for this, which is true in a broader sense.

Indeed, once anthropologists accept this kind of engagement, they must also think of the consequences for their fieldwork presence on a long term. I visited Oksapmin twice after the finishing of my surveying, each time for a few weeks. It was almost impossible to me to discuss any other topic than the mine. People looked definitively at me as one of those responsible for the system of compensation payments. In this frame, it is quite hard to come back to the quiet, classic way of carrying out fieldwork.

As a final reflection I would say that, with all its difficulties, this experience has enriched my approach to the fieldwork and changed my relation to it. I had the wish to work on something extremely real and important for the people, much more immediately important to them than the classic ethnographic topics I had inquired into before. In several cases, my relationship with the Oksapmin people I have worked with has become deeper and stronger. Maybe I am wrong, but I had the feeling that this was the first time I was useful to them.

Acknowledgments

I wish sincerely to thank Andrew Strathern and Pamela J. Stewart for their editorial work on this essay. As author, I remain responsible for any substantive shortcomings in it.

Notes

1. PNG National Census, 1995.
2. John Black made the first documented contact by Westerners with the Oksapmin people in July 1938. During the days of the first contact, four Oksapmin men died, killed by the patrol policemen to ward off a suspected attack. Owing to the problem the first patrol had with the local people but also to the difficult geomorphology of the Oksapmin territory, the first Australian settlement of the area was established in the Telefomin area, a much wider valley.
3. The Black-Taylor patrol (1938).

References

Brutti, L. 1997 "Waiting for God: Ecocosmological Transformations among the Oksapmin". In P.J. Stewart and A. Strathern (eds) *Millennial Markers*, pp. 87–131. Townsville: James Cook University, Centre for Pacific Studies.

———— 1999 "On His Holiness' Service: Representations of Catholicism in Contemporary Evangelised Papua New Guinea". In Christin Kocher Schmid (ed) *Expecting the Day of Wrath: Versions of the Millennium in Papua New Guinea*, pp. 44–56. Port Moresby: The National Research Institute.

Filer, C. 1999 "The Dialectics of Negation and Negotiation in the Anthropology of Mineral Resource Development in Papua New Guinea". In A. Cheater (ed) *The Anthropology of Power*, pp. 88–102. London: Routledge.

Robbins, J. 1995 "Dispossessing the Spirits: Christian Transformations of Desire and Ecology among the Urapmin of Papua New Guinea". *Ethnology* 34(3):211–224.

Chapter 6

TAKING CARE OF CULTURE
Consultancy, Anthropology, and Gender Issues

Martha Macintyre

In Papua New Guinea the use of anthropologists as consultants for government and development projects has a long and respectable history.
From the early colonial period there were official government anthropologists to colonial administrations whose ethnographic writings remain
'classics' and over the past sixty years many of the anthropologists who
have undertaken project consultancies have been also major figures in the
academic domain. The Papua New Guinea Research Unit (based at the
Australian National University) during the 1970s and 1980s produced
some fine anthropological work that was directed toward dealing with the
practical problems of economic development and what is now called governance, but was then termed government and administration.

This relationship, in Melanesia and elsewhere, has since the 1960s been
the subject of intense criticism within the discipline (Asad 1973; Clifford
1988). The idea that Anthropology as a discipline is tainted when it becomes an instrument in developing strategies for administering aid or
working out sustainable development projects jostles with the criticisms
that many anthropologists make of projects that they fail because they do
not take into account the cultural specificities and deeply rooted values of
the people. Accusations of complicity with oppressive policies or exploitative economics are commonplace. In this chapter I shall examine a few of
the ways that my work as a consultant has impinged on my academic
research, and inspired some criticisms of my academic discipline, but I
shall also argue for the usefulness of anthropology in undertaking social
research that has very practical aims.

Sometimes anthropologists I speak with bemoan the lack of influence
that the discipline has outside the academic domain. In fact, I encounter

References for this chapter are located on page 138.

traces of (usually somewhat dated) anthropological debates constantly in the terms of reference, reports, and guidelines of development projects. One of the clichés of anthropological critiques of development projects, now thoroughly incorporated into the language of aid agencies and non-governmental organizations working in the Pacific, is the concept of 'cultural appropriateness'. I do not contest the need for developers to be aware of the cultures of the people whose resources they are exploiting, but the issue becomes decidedly more complicated when you actually try to work with that in mind as a way of determining policy and practice. Presumably, that is one reason why anthropologists are hired as consultants to assist at the various stages of planning and implementation so that the project will be successful. Deciding on those aspects of a project that are likely to be in conflict with pervasive cultural values is much more difficult than recognizing the problem areas after the fact. The social sciences generally are not predictive, and Papua New Guinean people change their minds about the things that are important to them.

The first time that I was approached to undertake a social impact assessment for a mining project I accepted because I thought that I would be able to provide informed recommendations based on an anthropological study. As the project site was Misima and I had some knowledge of the region, I felt that by putting my knowledge to some useful end, I could in some way 'pay a debt' to the people of Milne Bay who had provided me with hospitality, and shared their knowledge and understandings with me as I did fieldwork over the previous eight years. While I do not subscribe to the view that anthropological research is an exploitative or selfish activity, nor that anthropologists rarely return the favors that they have been given, the opportunity to apply my discipline to constructive ends appealed.

Having taught subjects that dealt with the effects of economic change on women's lives I also hoped that I would be able to discuss the social impact issues with women and to incorporate their aspirations into recommendations about community involvement. Criticisms often made of development interventions are that they fail to take into account the values that women hold and that in introducing new ways of attaining wealth and status, projects erode traditions that secured for women recognition and value within their communities. The other oft-repeated observation is that men are given privileged access to new wealth and status so that women are doubly disadvantaged.

Working in communities such as Misima, where I had some familiarity with the ways that men and women communicated and cooperated, was relatively easy. I knew the sorts of occasions when it was appropriate to discuss things with a group of women and when I'd have to do numerous household interviews. I knew that some topics were best dealt with in individual conversations and others would generate enthusiastic discussion. Knowing the strength of the women's church organizations in Milne Bay Province also meant that having talked to a few women leaders, they would decide on the best mode of eliciting women's views and organize my work accordingly.

Women, like men, usually want access to money. Often they are enthusiastic about being employed. On both Misima and Lihir (New Ireland) men believed that they were entitled to jobs generated by the mining project and that women were not. On Misima there was far greater acceptance that women who had been educated should be engaged in wage labor, but great resistance to 'village' women working. Two reasons predominate and they are sometimes unabashedly articulated—the fear that women will engage in illicit sexual relationships once they are away from the constraints of village life, and male antagonism toward the economic autonomy that women have when they earn money.

On Misima both men and women voiced fears about the breakdown of sexual morality, in public meetings and in private conversations. On Lihir, where I had far more research time over a two-year period to interview a statistically representative number of people, it was clear that many more men opposed female employment on those grounds. Women thought that the work environment would provide opportunities for sexual liaisons that did not exist when women were in the village, but only 10 percent thought that they therefore should not be employed. The objection to female employment on the grounds that they become more independent was almost exclusively male on both Misima and Lihir. On both islands most women believed that this would happen, and this was the basis for their enthusiasm for employment. In each place, I believe if a plebiscite of public views on the matter had been taken, the small number of men and the large number of women would have constituted a clear majority. But in this instance 'culture' rather than democracy triumphed. The 'work culture' of mining and the dominance of Papua New Guinean men in representative forums ensured that women would not be employed in jobs that men saw as 'masculine'.

There are not usually many jobs for women in mining projects. In Australia (where equal opportunity legislation exists) in 1996 women constituted only 4 percent of the workforce on mine sites. Female geologists and engineers tend to work for relatively short periods of time, and in one study the overwhelming majority of women interviewed reported that they experienced sexual discrimination in the workplace (Pattenden 1996). As many of the expatriates recruited to work in Papua New Guinea come from Australia, the attitudes and practices are similar. Men who have not happily adopted policies that incorporate women into their working environment elsewhere do not suddenly transform in Papua New Guinea. Given that local men are hostile to women's employment, those who are not really comfortable with equal opportunity in Australia then shore up their prejudices by appealing to 'cultural sensitivity'. Almost all the Papua New Guineans they meet reinforce the view that women should not be employed.

The representatives of mining companies who negotiate leases with government and local people are invariably male. The Papua New Guinean politicians, public servants and community representatives are also male. Both groups are often very conservative about gender roles. In Papua New Guinea there are very few women with the technical or professional qualifications needed on mining sites. The most highly paid women are usually those with secretarial or administrative positions. The education system, the fact that many of the churches have reactionary ideas on the social roles of women, and the pervasive view that feminist objectives (or arguments about gender equity) are the province of foreign sexual libertarians, all combine to ensure that innovative employment policies are rejected by most men and many educated women.

Women whose lives have been circumscribed by the demands of subsistence agriculture and village life are often far more adventurous. Not having been exposed to some of the stereotypes of gender and modern work, in interviews they expressed enthusiasm for training in driving vehicles or operating machinery and learning various trade skills. This openness evaporated during the construction phase when they observed very few expatriate women doing such jobs and the mine was clearly defined as a masculine place.

A few Lihirian women persevered and were supported by senior management in both the mining company and the local umbrella company, Lakaka. An expatriate woman was employed to teach driving of heavy vehicles and this undoubtedly moderated the views of some people. But given the prestige that Papua New Guinean men associate with driving trucks, women trainees had a difficult time.

Lihirian men objected to women driving vehicles because they considered it men's work and they wanted all driving jobs. They appealed to customs in ways that were dogmatic and imaginative. As is often the case in anthropological research, the debate facilitated a far better ethnographic understanding of gender and pollution than any direct questions would have generated. Their arguments provided very detailed information on men's understanding of the ways that menstrual pollution worked.

Actual contact with menstrual blood would weaken men and decrease their physical strength. Women therefore should not be allowed to drive because they would pollute the vehicle if they were menstruating, making it dangerous for men to sit in the same seat. But their polluting powers were even more insidious, as they would emanate from their bodies through the expenditure of energy and so permeate the fluids in the engine. This idea was extrapolated from ideas of work and waste that possibly represent an earlier syncretic association (from traditional concepts and basic biological education) between body waste and danger whereby sweat can transmit hazardous substances. The view presented entailed an idea of the machine and operator working together and thereby mutually producing fluids and heat as waste (the analogy being that traditionally women could not use

men's axes, knives or spears because of this process). The heat and sweat
from the woman driver would infuse the oil circulating in the machine and
thus make the engine dysfunctional when men used the vehicle. Finally
they produced their 'trump card': the sump, as the repository of machine
and female waste products would be filled with hazardous waste that
would endanger the lives of the mechanics who had to dispose of it when
they serviced the vehicles.

The ingenuity of their argument delighted me, but I wondered how
much was simply impromptu and fanciful extrapolation, as the men were
aware already that an appeal to 'kastom' always seemed to impress outsiders. Familiar with a smattering of English terms related to the work,
their explanations coupled substances that were 'nogut' and 'pipia' with
'danger', 'unsafe practices' and 'hazardous waste products'. Chemical waste
and air pollution, ideas encountered in discussions about the environmental impact of the mine, were equated with the potent emanations from
female Lihirian bodies. The two Lihirian women with me appeared to be at
a loss for answers to these objections in spite of their vehemence about
women having access to work and training. When I suggested that women
be trained to be mechanics so that men and machines (women and their
tools not being subject to such dangers) not be placed in jeopardy, they
countered with the argument they considered unassailable: women could
not be mechanics as that would require that they wear trousers.

I was somewhat surprised when my questions about the dangers of
women driving were confirmed by village men, at least in the matter of
heat, sweat and blood being 'dirty' and hazardous to men. Women appeared equally alarmed at the prospect of men being harmed if menstruating women were operating equipment. A few dismissed these ideas as
superstitious, but only a handful of women were prepared to uphold any
ideas of gender equity in the face of men's arguments.

Similar fears had been voiced in 1995 about the design of relocation
houses. People maintained that if they were on stilts then women might
walk around the house while men were seated below—a gross breach of
respect (being above men) as well as a an infringement of pollution rules.
However, in that instance men's desires for houses that were large and
looked like those belonging to senior public servants in Kavieng (the
provincial capital) overcame their fears of polluting women and they
insisted on houses on stilts. The opportunistic invocation of 'kastom' to
exclude women and the abandonment of traditional practices in favor of
ideas about prestige and display of benefits reveal the strategic use of
notions of 'cultural sensitivity' by Lihirian men. Their privileged access to
the company and their confidence in public discussions mean that their
voices are heard and their interpretations of custom (however malleable
or strategic) are attended to more often than those of women.

While the opportunity to employ women in a wide range of jobs was
missed, Lihirian women have in some respects taken advantage of the

traditions of gender distinction that gave them some control over their economic activities. Male fears of female sexual and economic autonomy were well-founded. Women who work are less likely to marry if they become pregnant. They might sue the father of the child for maintenance if he is employed—but they will not succumb to parental pressure to marry. They resist giving money to men. Often resistance is unsuccessful—especially if a customary feast is occurring—but most young working women make independent decisions about income disposal and few give any money to men. Four years after the village meetings in which men harangued me, the community relations department and all women in attendance about the horrors of women wearing trousers, young working women and their village sisters wear them regularly. Now men grudgingly accept these developments as part of the changes that bring them benefits.

Women are consulted by anthropologists, they do not participate in negotiations. The predominance of men in public life and the desire of Melanesian men to control economic benefits ensure that very few of the 'lessons learned' from anthropological studies ever influence policies. The changes in gender roles and the transformations in the sexual division of labor that occur in the context of resource extractive industries are dramatic, swift and usually disadvantage women (Bonnell 1997; Macintyre 1993; Polier 1992). But the power relations, with respect to gender, are not altered because of attention to cultural sensibilities, as men are the people 'in the community' whose representations are accepted as authoritative.

Sensitivity to diverse cultural beliefs and practices is in itself an idea derived from Western twentieth-century liberalism. In Australia and other countries such as Canada, where multi-culturalism has been adopted as government policy, the idea of 'culture' that operates stresses difference and exoticism when selecting aspects of culture that should be protected or encouraged. Working within this framework, expatriate employers are often much more willing to take note of customs that are unique, colorful or strange than they are to accept or accommodate traditions that really require fundamental changes in approach to employment regulations. For example, prolonged funeral ceremonies and Melanesians who are unfortunate enough to have three mothers die in a relatively short period of time are dealt with skeptically. As both Misima and Lihir people have matrilineal kinship systems, on several occasions I have had lengthy discussions with departmental heads who ask me to explain just how a person can have three mothers. The majority remain adamant that they 'don't mind them taking three days off for their mother's funeral but feel as if they are being duped when 'it is *really* an aunt or a distant cousin'. Being a cultural interpreter is in many respects one of the most enjoyable parts of consulting work. Sometimes it is useful in preventing conflict or discontent.

But as with the matter of houses and trousers on Lihir, often the anthropologist might end up arguing for cultural sensitivity toward a customary practice that local people find loses its meaning in the context of modern living. On Misima in 1986, as elsewhere in Milne Bay Province, postpartum food taboos and customs of ritual purification were routinely observed by the majority of village women. A crucial part of these entailed women bathing in the sea and consuming several liters of seawater each day over a period of weeks after a birth. As mining activities were going to cause large quantities of silt to flow into sea water near the villages adjacent to the mine, I canvassed the opinions of women about the need to continue these rituals and alternative ways of performing the seawater cleansing. The mining company was prepared to install saltwater showers and to assist in any way that was acceptable to the women.

I sought information on the possible beneficial effects of the practice, discovering that the clear, blue seawater harbored large numbers of *e.coli* and other bacteria and that the consumption of large amounts of it internally would distend the belly and possibly be a contributing factor in later uterine prolapse. I presented this information to women at village meetings and they insisted that regardless of what medical science thought of their practices they were crucial to the well-being of newly delivered mothers and babies. We formed a small committee that devised a range of options that appeared to satisfy local women and the company did its best to provide these alternatives.

Within a year the practice was virtually abandoned in villages near the mine site and many women objected more to the fuss that the company community relations officers made about saltwater bathing facilities than they did to the silting damage to their beaches. The 'cultural value' that endured was that of female modesty about childbirth, not belief in the efficacy of taboos. They did not think their health was jeopardized by the abandonment of these customs. Having a hospital, more maternal health care and houses with bathrooms altered the ways that women thought about the rituals of purification and they embraced the new ways of ensuring their recovery from birth without any regrets for the past. Several women I spoke with in 1993 commented that drinking draughts of seawater was an unpleasant task and that they were glad the requirement had gone.

The attraction of 'protecting' or being sensitive to the exotic rather than responding to the mundane needs of women during a period of great socio-economic change can in many respects be a diversion. These examples indicate the ways that apparently entrenched ideas about women's roles and status can be subject to very rapid modification and even discarded without the women themselves experiencing the demise as a loss or even feeling regret.

The work of assisting in developing policies that are aimed at avoiding conflict underlies many social impact consultancies. The expectation that the most disruptive conflict will be between the mining company and the community informs most terms of reference. But the assumption of Melanesian communalism is more often the blight of many development projects.

Conflict with the company can be dramatic and disruptive, but conflict within the community is corrosive and the source of many of the social problems that emerge and become entrenched.

When I undertook the first consultancy I had some idea of the areas that might be examined, but prepared myself by immersing myself in the literature on other mining projects in developing countries. Given that the Bougainville conflict had to some extent inspired my appointment, I read all I could find in the hope of developing strategies that avoided the conflicts generated there. I tracked down some of the Australian people who had worked for Bougainville Copper and asked for their opinions about the ways that things could have been done to avoid the problems that arose. I contacted Bougainvilleans living in Port Moresby and Alotau and discussed their perceptions of the sources of conflict and their ideas about the ways such conflict might have been avoided.

In retrospect my approach might appear innocently optimistic. In fact the voracious reading spree that took me from Katanga in Africa, via numerous mine sites in South America and SE Asia, to Panguna in Melanesia provided me with an understanding of the social and economic impact of mining projects that continues to inform my work. As with most academic research, the recurring patterns often emerge only when you read numerous versions of similar situations. While not all the communities described experienced major violent conflict, most were riven with tensions between those who benefited and those who perceived themselves to have missed out. In every instance those who see themselves as deprived invoke images of village life as harmonious and communal. The appeal to a romanticized past where *communitas* reigned and all social relations were equitable and just emerges as a way of representing the world that has been lost. Thus it is that the rhetoric of relative deprivation merges with those conventions of anthropology that have as their subject a community that is an abstract but unified entity: a 'society' with a 'culture'.

The tensions between the political rhetoric of Papua New Guineans whose anguish about emerging inequalities is expressed in a nostalgia for a past that never existed, and the anthropological representation of the current political, social and cultural turmoil as delightfully 'hybrid' are extreme. Working in the area of 'gender' or on issues affecting women in contemporary Papua New Guinea, similar oppositions are obvious. I occasionally feel quite alienated from the ways that academic feminism determines the subject of women's lives. For while there is acknowledgement of the need to listen to the voices of women themselves, when they say things that do not 'fit' current ideas of 'difference', they are ignored as subjects of interest. This has been most noticeable in working on an Australian aid project aimed at improving community relations with police and advancing the careers of women police. On the police project my work is mainly in towns, in police stations and with women from 'settlements' as well as women's organizations. My work with women police, for example, reveals that women mostly voice their discontents in terms of discriminatory promotion policies, low wages, sexist attitudes from male colleagues and the trials of having the double burden of housework and a job. Their ethnic origins and cultural differences are irrelevant as they see that their interests will only be advanced by uniting in a struggle against the pervasive male chauvinism of men in the police force. Occasionally, they enjoy discussing 'customs' and regional variations—but usually in the context of pointing out the basic similarities of female experience across Papua New Guinea. They scoff when I proffer relativist arguments about bride price, but they sometimes seize on fantasies of a golden past that their grandmothers enjoyed, when 'custom' prevailed and women were 'respected'.

Sometimes, when I have aired some anthropological interpretation of a female initiation ceremony or a marriage ritual as indicative of the complementary (valued) role of women in the past they simply sit and look at me with cynical stares. One woman commented to me, "You anthropologists, I don't trust that sort of talk. It sounds like my father trying to get me married to some man who offered a big bride price".

The suspicion directed at academics who work as consultants, at least in the social sciences, comes from all sides. While I enjoy my discussions with police women and women whose lives are being transformed by large mining projects, the criticism from colleagues and bureaucrats is less congenial. It often provides me with anthropological musings about territoriality and the need to demarcate clear boundaries between us/them. Consultant anthropologists occupy the liminal zone much of the time— with bureaucrats apparently resentful of them as trespassers and fellow academics suspicious that they are debasing the currency.

Having worked as a 'consultant', who does research, writes reports, and makes recommendations, and as a member of a project team, who has to train, advise, and implement a project, I often share the skepticism toward 'academic' understandings of a situation. But this has stimulated my interest in the 'depoliticization' of critical anthropology, rather than made me feel that anthropology is irrelevant. This is particularly true in respect to the study of women in developing countries. In the case of Papua New Guinea, where women's health, education, and employment prospects have barely moved over twenty-five years of independence, the 'usefulness' of anthropological research is clear.

The alleged gap between 'academic' and 'practical' understandings of socio-economic situations is often appealed to by people who work in government and non-government agencies. In my experience, most bureaucrats working in government are profoundly anti-intellectual, the exceptions being those (who are usually in senior positions) who have high academic qualifications themselves. My encounters with industrial employers have been somewhat different, for they seem more often to hire consultants as experts in their fields and so adopt a more business-like relationship. The major difficulties arise around issues of intellectual property and confidentiality, although this usually centers on the document produced rather than the 'information' as an abstraction. But there is a strong view within universities that working in 'applied' fields is not only ethically suspect, but constitutes an abandonment of all theoretical interests or commitment to scholarly debate. One result of this is the relinquishment of teaching the anthropology of social impact analysis to programs within universities that are vocationally oriented and where the training tends to be programmatic and superficial.

Social and environmental impact assessment is, on the face of it, the sort of task that can be well managed by an anthropologist. The range of issues that must be examined, the need to explore the interactions and relationships between people, their environments, and the processes of transformation associated with economic change have long been subjects of anthropological research. The social and cultural changes associated with colonialism and modernization have been central to the discipline of anthropology for over fifty years.

Whenever I attend meetings or seminars where I encounter NGO bureaucrats or management companies who present neat 'log frames' and survey sheets that are meant to provide measurable indicators of impact or social risk I am usually left speechless by their naiveté. The superficiality of most procedures aimed at 'assessing' and the blind faith that many corporations appear to have in facile grids with coded evaluations is disturbing. In the end however the desire for reductionist analysis is confounded by the complexity of the situations they are confronted by.

Yet in working as a consultant, I am often struck by the tensions between the requirements of a report, the questions it needs to address and my interests as an anthropologist. The terms of reference for a report are necessarily restricted and the research is constrained by other factors such as the brevity of fieldwork, the problem areas identified by the client and the community, and the need to communicate information to people without using the jargon or language of one's discipline.

This latter constraint is partly self-imposed and partly a response to that pervasive anti-intellectualism of bureaucrats in both non-government and government agencies.

The ethical dilemmas facing anthropologists, who are accustomed to identifying themselves with the interests of the communities in which they have undertaken research, have been discussed extensively in the context of 'applied anthropology'. For many the emphasis is on the problematic positions of advocate or observer. The advocacy role fits well with some of the work to be done in a social impact study. But often it assumes a community that is homogenous, united and politically able to oppose activities by a mining or logging company whose presence is endorsed by the state. This happened briefly on Bougainville, but very rapidly the 'community' divided into warring factions.

In most Papua New Guinea communities where development projects occur, the social, economic and political splits in the communities affected are immediately obvious. Over time they change as different interests are formulated and people realign themselves, or as new leaders and factions emerge. Only those who willfully cling to a primitivist image of villagers living in harmony with each other and their natural environment could clearly identify themselves as 'advocates' for the community they work in. The 'community' is most often a political fiction, with little of the harmony or unity that enable a person to be positioned as advocate for a cohesive, clearly identifiable group. Besides, the company, the government and the local people have all designated entirely different roles for the anthropological consultant and negotiating the different expectations creates even more complicated dilemmas. In my experience, the most complex ethical issues do not involve my academic discipline at all, rather they present as differences in aims, political allegiances and ideas about future equity and stability. In Papua New Guinea they emerge as one confronts the fact that women are disadvantaged, discriminated against and are being excluded from decision-making by their men.

At present, large multi-national companies (especially those engaged in resource extraction in developing countries such as Papua New Guinea) are under great pressure from human rights and environmental activists in Europe and America to demonstrate their commitment to social and environmental sustainability. The environmental damage caused by mining and deforestation in the nineteenth and twentieth centuries is now recognized by Europeans, Americans and Australians—those who have benefited most from these activities. In Australia and America particularly, the ghost towns and bare mullock heaps, the barren landscapes of abandoned pits, and the forests laid waste by the fumes of smelters or cleared for agriculture are sad reminders of the costs of their nation's industrial progress. The sense of loss, the increased awareness of the long-term consequences of resource extraction, and fear of even more dire environmental damage have inspired political action aimed at limiting (or preventing) further destruction. But as miners and loggers are wont to observe, these people live in nations where the demand for goods produced from these resources remains undiminished.

The pressures on mining companies to improve their performance by limiting environmental damage increased, and many of the large multi-nationals were convinced that there were economic advantages in doing so. Regulation and technological advances were combined with careful monitoring to this end. The adverse social and political effects of mining projects in undeveloped countries, while well documented by anthropologists and others, are not so readily accepted. But gradually the social disintegration and political turmoil that has been observed—particularly in African and South American countries where resource extraction by foreign companies was careless of the long-term consequences—have become liabilities. Over the last decade many companies, as well as the nations that encourage their activities in the interests of economic development, have embraced policies that are intended to reduce negative social impacts and enhance community development.

The issue that is most striking in working with these companies and organizations is the lack of familiarity with social science. Not surprisingly, this is most obvious in mining companies where the boards and managers are usually professionals whose disciplines are technical, scientific or financial. Accustomed to dealing with research on inanimate objects or abstractions, one of the most difficult problems I have had is conveying the reasons why anthropological research takes so much time (eight weeks of fieldwork are considered a lot to collect all information on social impact in a population of 10,000). But there is an even more difficult area, the fact that social problems (especially those arising in the context of rapid industrialization and economic change in remote rural areas) do not have single causes, and that identification of a problem does not mean that the mining company has somehow knowingly and intentionally inflicted harm on the population. The problems of sexual discrimination, of ways that mining companies and other developers are complicit by default in the disadvantaging of women, are perhaps the most difficult to deal with in ways that are comprehensible.

Alcohol problems are the most complex to explain. On Misima and on Lihir, beer consumption has caused major social problems. Having documented the way that beer is implicated in a very high accident and injury rate, in violence, impoverishment, family breakdown, and constant disturbance of the peace in villages, I was told, "Well we don't pour it down their throats! It's not our responsibility". Similarly, in pointing out the need for social welfare, I was told firmly by one manager, "I run a mining company, not a bloody philanthropic society". It is very easy to persuade the company to respond to simple issues of commission or omission, but hard work explaining the complexities of social impact when the most negative effects are due to the ways that Papua New Guineans choose to use and display their new found affluence.

The rise in violent crime on Lihir and other project sites in PNG can in many respects be attributed to the ways that Papua New Guinean men behave when drunk. The resort to violence in arguments between men was rare before the mining project began, and became commonplace during the construction phase in 1995–1996 when most young Lihirian men were employed. But it must also be understood as an expression of the new divisions created by the inequitable distribution of benefits—for this has provided new grounds for conflict. The disinhibiting effects of alcohol enable men to abandon the social constraints that normally (traditionally?) suppress confrontation and men concede that they sometimes drink in order to be able to express frustrations and jealousies that would be otherwise inadmissible in a small village. Beer drinking and its social impacts are extraordinarily convoluted.

Anthropological explanations engage with this complexity. I have always been suspicious of claims about the 'scientific' nature of anthropological inquiry and the multiplicity of theoretical approaches to the study of social and cultural behavior offer far more scope for interpretation. The issues of 'drunken comportment', rituals of male sociality in Melanesia, the ways that men incorporate beer into exchanges that gain them prestige—these render the profligate expenditure on beer and the 'anti-social' behavior comprehensible. But they also make it difficult to present simple solutions that can be condensed into 'recommendations' for actions on the part of the company. This is perhaps one of the reasons why corporations are sometimes suspicious of anthropologists and are susceptible to the promise of 'social impact' analysis in the form of quick surveys that generate numerical assessments of 'risk' or stability.

The transformation of social analysis into a series of set questions and answers began as a management tool. As corporatism has taken hold in government bureaucracies, the 'business' of social impact analysis or monitoring has been subjected to many of the same constraints that academics encounter in processes of performance 'measurement' or teaching 'evaluation' logical frameworks, grid patterns with every component of a project set down under a heading. Achievements or successes are assessed in terms of 'verifiable indicators' and levels of success allotted points denote 'quality'. These methods of reporting, assessing or documenting are at present in vogue with non-governmental organizations, government agencies, and some companies. By attaching numbers to qualitative judgments, they provide bureaucrats with the illusion of measurable achievement and endow reports with a scientistic certainty. These measurements are almost always spurious. Based on models of economic processes, they reduce human activity and social processes to inputs and outputs, while assigning human agency to the boxes for 'assumptions' and 'risks'. People become 'stakeholders', recipients of aid become 'partners', and those who have to work on aid projects spend at least half of their time writing reports and filling out boxes on grids.

The advantage of coming into this world as an anthropologist is that it enables one to place this cumbersome reductionism in historical perspective, and to recognize its jargon as a discursive ploy. Ironies abound. In projects that are aimed at improving women's economic status or education or participation in political decisions, the inertia and antagonism of men (whose privileges are vested in the complex historical cultural traditions entitling them to control women) are reduced to a 'risk factor' that has to be summarized to fit the cell in a grid, in perhaps ten words. While I am sometimes inspired to write a novel that would parody the aid and consultancy businesses, I draw comfort from the fact that management systems alter very quickly. The failure of these methods will become apparent within a few years and the inflexibility they impose will be recognized as an impediment to the goals of the donors/recipients/partners who have to demonstrate that money is well spent. At present the confusion of accounting procedures with accountability has gained ground.

But consultancy research raises questions about the issues that absorb and inspire academic anthropology. Working within communities and institutions as they are changing, observing the debates and conflicts that rage between Papua New Guineans, and struggling to represent these varied interests in a relatively brief written report forces one to confront the problems of difference and purpose. While academics delight in the diversity and hybridity of Melanesian religious cults and practices, noting the imaginative blend of Western, traditional, and global elements, communities struggle with the social disruption and internal conflicts they generate. As a consultant, one is often forced to make judgements and align oneself with people who are upholding values that, as an anthropologist, one recognizes as 'foreign', and perhaps even alien to Melanesian cultural traditions. The most obvious dilemmas arise when basic human rights are denied to women and children.

I am no longer able to view the actions of men in 'tribal warfare' as having any legitimacy. The social costs are too great. My work on issues relating to the 'law and order' problems has compromised any anthropological moral relativism I might have embraced intellectually, beyond redemption. The violent behavior of men toward women in Papua New Guinea now draws on a range of 'traditional' justifications and incorporates bizarre and cruel actions derived from their understandings of the ways 'Western' culture heroes such as Rambo can kill with impunity.

Police have to deal with the problem of an initiation cult that 'revives' practices of group sexual access to a 'chosen' young woman. Some of her treatment is also inspired by Asian pornographic movies, and she is eventually found in the bush cult house in a deranged mental state, infected with gonorrhea, in a country where there are few psychiatric services and the health services in rural areas are often unable to supply basic medical attention because of inadequate funding. The woman's suffering, the inadequacies of state responses, the angry response toward the young men who were members of the cult—all of these matters have an urgency that demands political and practical reaction. My interest in the cultural elements of this particular male cult is rapidly eclipsed by my concern that yet another Papua New Guinean woman who has been subjected to pack rape has no chance of receiving psychiatric counseling and may even find that the health center she is taken to has no supply of antibiotics.

Being 'on the ground' with police or health service providers, or villagers who are dealing with unprecedented levels of alcohol related violence, changes the ways that one engages with academic anthropological research. Working as a consultant on a variety of projects has provided me with opportunities to work 'cross-culturally' within Papua New Guinea that would have been impossible had I remained an 'academic' researcher. My experiences in towns, villages, mine sites, police stations, hospitals and attending meetings of women's organizations sometimes make me dismissive of the arcane arguments of my discipline. But more often I find that the most complicated and confronting issues are only illuminated or rendered comprehensible by 'applying anthropology'.

References

Asad, T. (ed) 1973 *Anthropology and the Colonial Encounter.* London: Ithaca Press.

Bonnell, S. 1997 "The Impact of Compensation and Relocation on Marriage in Porgera". In Susan Toft (ed) *Compensation for Resource Development in Papua New Guinea*, pp. 137–142. Canberra: Law Reform Commission of PNG, Monograph No. 6, and National Centre for Development Studies.

Clifford, J. 1988 *The Predicament of Culture: Twentieth-Century Ethnography, Literature and Art.* Cambridge, Mass.: Harvard University Press.

Macintyre, M. 1993 "Women and Mining". In *Papua New Guinea and Australia—Towards 2000*, pp. 43–49. Fitzroy: Conference papers published by Community Aid Abroad.

Pattenden, C. 1996 "Women in the Minerals Industry in Australia". Report prepared for the Australian Mining Industry Institute.

Polier, N. 1996 "Of Mines and Min: Modernity and Its Malcontents in Papua New Guinea". *Ethnology* 35(1):1–16.

CONTRIBUTORS

Lorenzo Brutti is an anthropologist at the Centre National de la Recherche Scientifique in Paris, where he is working in the scientific multi-media program of the forthcoming Musée du Quai Branly, and he has been the project manager of the multi-media scientific room dedicated to Arts of Asia, Africa, Oceania, and the Americas at the Musée du Louvre. He teaches anthropology at the Institut Scientifique et Technique d'Outre Mer in Cergy Pontoise and is consultant for the UNESCO program "Masterpieces of Intangible Heritage of Humanity". He has recently published *La terra dei miei sogni. Esperienze di ricerca in Oceania* (Roma: Meltemi); "L'anthropologie est-elle soluble dans l'art premier? Essai de lecture ethnographique du Musée du Quai Branly par le regard d'un observateur participant", in *Esthétiques: Europe, Chine et ailleurs* (Paris: You Feng); "Le donneur, le receveur et la sage-femme. Echanges de cochons à Oksapmin, Papouasie Nouvelle Guinée" (*Journal de la Société des Océanistes*); and "Aprés nous le déluge". Les effets de la présence d'une compagnie minière sur le système agricole et le commerce des produits cultivés dans la région d'Oksapmin, Papouasie Nouvelle Guinée" (*Journal of Applied Tropical and Botanical Agriculture*).

Martha Macintyre is a Senior Lecturer at the Centre for the Study of Health and Society at the University of Melbourne. She also works as a consultant anthropologist in Papua New Guinea, where she has been monitoring the social impact of the gold mining project on Lihir in New Ireland province over the past decade. She has worked on several Australian aid projects as a designer, in-country advisor, and evaluator. She has published numerous articles on women and gender relations in Papua New Guinea and was an editor of the volume *Human Rights and Gender Politics: Asia-Pacific Perspectives* (Routledge, 2000).

Marta A. Rohatynskyj teaches in the Department of Anthropology at the University of Guelph. She has worked as a consultant and has conducted academic research in both West Africa and Papua New Guinea. She has published in anthropological journals and is co-editor, with Sjoerd R. Jaarsma, of *Ethnographic Artifacts: Challenges to a Reflexive Anthropology*, published by University of Hawai'i Press.

Richard Scaglion is Professor and Chair of Anthropology at the University of Pittsburgh. His primary geographic interests lie in the Pacific Islands and insular Southeast Asia, where he specializes in Melanesia and in the comparative study of Austronesian societies. A recipient of a Praxis Award from the Washington Society for Professional Anthropologists, Scaglion's applied research has involved the anthropology of law and sustainable development in island nations. He has a special relationship with the Abelam people of New Guinea, with whom he has conducted long-term field research beginning in 1974. He is the former Director of Customary Law Development for the Law Reform Commission of Papua New Guinea and has been a Visiting Fellow at the Australian National University, the University of Hawai'i, and the East-West Center in Honolulu. He is editor of *Homicide Compensation in Papua New Guinea* and *Customary Law in Papua New Guinea*, and author of numerous other books and articles, including *The Globalization of Food* (Waveland Press, 2002).

Pamela J. Stewart and **Andrew Strathern** are research collaborators in the Department of Anthropology at the University of Pittsburgh. They have published many books and articles on their research in the Pacific, Europe, and Asia. They are co-editors for the *Journal of Ritual Studies*. Their most recent co-authored books include *Witchcraft, Sorcery, Rumors and Gossip* (Cambridge University Press, 2004), *Violence: Theory and Ethnography* (Continuum Publishing, 2002), and *Remaking the World: Myth, Mining, and Ritual Change among the Duna of Papua New Guinea* (Smithsonian Institution Press, 2002). Their most recent co-edited volumes include *Landscape, Memory, and History: Anthropological Perspectives* (Pluto Press, 2003) and *Identity Work: Constructing Pacific Lives* (University of Pittsburgh Press, 2000).

John R. Wagner is an Assistant Professor in the Department of Anthropology at Okanagan University College in Kelowna, British Columbia, Canada. He is also co-investigator for the Social Research for Sustainable Fisheries (SRSF) Project sited at St. Francis Xavier University in Antigonish, Nova Scotia. He has recently co-authored a number of journal publications with SRSF Director Anthony Davis and other SRSF partners on the subjects of local ecological knowledge (*Human Ecology* 31[3]), property rights in the Nova Scotia lobster fishery (forthcoming in *Human Organization*), and the cultural and ecological relationship of the Mi'kmaq people to the American eel (forthcoming in *Native Studies*). He continues to pursue his research interests in Kamu Yali and Papua New Guinea, and his works in progress include an edited volume on issues of property and ecology in the Pacific. He is also engaged in the first phase of a long-term collaborative research project in the Okanagan region of British Columbia on the theme of Okanagan social and ecological history.

Paige West is an Assistant Professor in the Department of Anthropology at Barnard College and is on the Graduate Faculty in the Department of Anthropology and the Department of Ecology, Evolution, and Environmental Biology at Columbia University. She has conducted research in Papua New Guinea and in the United States. In 2002 she received the American Anthropological Association's Anthropology and Environment Junior Scholar award, and she has recently completed a manuscript entitled "Conservation Is Our Government Now: Integrated Conservation and Development Interventions in the Eastern Highlands of Papua New Guinea", which will be published by Duke University Press. She is currently working on a second manuscript entitled "Coffee, Gold, and Souls: Commodity Chains and Environmental Change in Papua New Guinea".

INDEX